Environmental Laws
Of
India

I0477067

Harkanwal Singh
Shipali Rani

ISBN: 1512068470
ISBN: 978-1512068474
First Edition 2015
© Harkanwal singh

PREFACE

As a country, we have made substantial progress in cleaning up the environment, thanks to the ambitious statutory frame work, impressive contributions by states, municipalities, and the private sector, and most importantly by the Indian Public's unwavering support for clean air and water. And yet, we face a daunting array of challenges. The environment continues to be degraded by toxic chemicals such as pesticides, heavy metals and synthetic organic compounds. We continue to lose wet lands, wildlife habitat and other productive natural resources to development. Demand has exploded for clean water for all its many purposes, in some places outstripping available supplies, as population and economic activity increase. We are notoriously inefficient in the way we use both water and energy. Numerous fisheries are excessively harvested or depleted, and coastal estuaries and waterways are degraded by runoff from sources of pollution dispersed across the landscape. Most obvious today is the threat of global climate change; as more green house gases are pumped into the atmosphere, leading scientists report we have reached, or be close to reaching , a "tipping point" that requires urgent action.

It is the time to rethink the roles and strategies of government and the private sector in safeguarding public health and the environment? Taking the twin pillars of regulation and enforcement as a foundation, tackling the challenges of global climate change and toxic pollution requires more of us to fashion nonpartisan solutions that enlist the creativity and entrepreneurial spirit of Indians. Technology, which has contributed to past problem, must be employed to reverse current energy and pollution trends, as they pose a clear risk to all of us. This requires the intelligent use of legal and economic tools to create appropriate incentives for those engaged in industry, agriculture, transportation, and business- as well as for consumers, and citizens generally- for we have learned over more than 30 years in this endeavour that environment protection is by no means the exclusive province of EPA. Rather, we have to build the concern into all aspects of our economic and community life if we are to achieve a safe, healthy environment.

We need far more attention devoted to the means by which we can stimulate and deploy new, more environmentally sustainable technologies. We need to harness market forces on behalf of the environment. More and more companies are learning that improving efficiency and cutting waste pays off – in their bottom line. Ultimately, we need to reconcile consumer demand with the growing awareness of its impacts on a finite and, it seems, increasingly vulnerable planet.

Environmental Laws of India provides a valuable foundation for constructing multifaceted approaches to nonpartisan environmentalism. It offers, in one place, grounding in environmental law, and policy. My hope is that this work will help provide the basis for renewing our commitment to environmental health in step with a modern industrial society. Our future may well depend on our ability to embrace a paradigm shift to sustainable development, in other words, to a model of economics prosperity that respects the essential contribution of natural systems on which all human activities depend.

Harkanwal singh
Shipali Rani

CONTENTS

1. ENVIRONMENTAL ISSUES AND PROBLEMS

An environmental problem arises whenever there is a change in the quality or quantity of any environmental factor which directly or indirectly affects the health and well-being of man in an adverse manner. Environmental problems can be studied from two different viewpoints. One is simply to look for adverse effects without regard to their origin in order to detect trends that call for further investigation; the other is to try to understand the cause and effect relationships, which make better prediction and proper management possible. Some of the environmental problems which are critical at the present time are fairly widely known because of the growing awareness of all levels of society, including governments, general public and the scientific community. However, our present information on the structure and function of the biosphere is not sufficient to allow an accurate evaluation of the total situation, expect to indicate some broad problem areas. There may be serious potential problems of which we are as yet unaware; other known problems may be less serious than we think. The Commission has made an extensive survey and analysis of those problems which are currently regarded as being of critical importance. The following criteria were used in an attempt to assess the critical nature of the problems to be solved in the near future:

a) Number of people and nations involved
b) Geographical distribution of the problem
c) Temporal distribution of the problem (temporary or long-term effects)
d) Degree of irreversibility of the effects
e) Degree of impact on health, standard of living, social structure and economy
f) Degree of international significance of the problem

Although these criteria overlap and may not be exhaustive, they form a useful basis for judgement. The consensus of the Commission's survey was that a fairly restricted number of problems were found to recur time and again. The major critical problem may be summarized as, "the adverse effects of a changed environment on human health and well-being"; i.e., the possibility that a changing environment may lead to increased mortality, increased frequency of diseases, lowered nutritional status via decreased agricultural productivity, or lowered psychological value of the environment. Concern has been widely expressed that these possible effects on man may be caused by direct input of toxic substances into the environment or improper land use. Climatic changes as a result of human activity may also adversely affect the standard of living through, for example reduced crop productivity, and increased energy consumption, etc.

Those problems considered most relevant for early implementation by a global environmental monitoring system are:

1. Potentially adverse climatic change resulting from human activities

2. Potentially adverse changes in biota and man from contamination by toxic substances including radio nuclides

3. Potentially adverse changes in biological productivity caused by improper land use (reduced soil fertility, soil erosion, extension of arid zones etc.)

A second category includes problems that, although of great importance, are not suitable for early global monitoring either because of their nature or because further study is necessary to determine whether they should be included in a global environmental monitoring system. These problems are:

4. Potentially adverse changes in the growth, structure and distribution of the human population

5. Changes in the subjective human perception of the environment

6. Eutrophication of waters

7. Decreasing freshwater resources

8. Natural disasters

DISCUSSION OF CRITIAL ENVIRONMENTAL PROBLEMS

1. Potentially Adverse Climatic Change Resulting from Human Activity

Large-scale climatic changes could be caused by alterations in the earth-atmosphere system through changes in: the atmospheric content of carbon dioxide; atmospheric turbidity (aerosol content); mean global cloudiness; the earth's surface; the composition of the stratosphere; and the amount of heat generated by man's activities. The concentration of atmospheric carbon dioxide is increasing at an average annual rate of nearly 0.3 percent. This increase, which is due to the burning of fossil fuels, is expected to accelerate in the future accompanying global economic development. Atmospheric carbon dioxide can influence climate through the "green-house effect", i.e. it is transparent to incoming solar radiation but partially absorbs the outgoing longer wavelength energy emitted by the earth. The best current estimates suggest that by 2000 A.D. the effect of increased CO_2 alone will be an average warming of the global surface temperature by roughly 0,5°C. Atmospheric aerosols attenuate solar radiation by absorbing and scattering (re-directing) it and are thereby potentially capable of affecting local and global climate. The nature of the climate change (warming or cooling) depends on the relative importance of these two radiative processes as well as the character of the earth's surface. In addition, atmospheric particles can affect the physical processes of precipitation and cloud formation through their role as condensation nuclei. Recent estimates have indicated that on a global basis, man's production of atmospheric particles is now roughly 10 to 50 percent of the natural rate. Locally, of course, the man-made contribution may far exceed that occurring naturally. Changes in the earth's reflectivity (albedo) are dominated by variations in cloudiness. Thus, any activity of man that affects large-scale cloudiness is likely to have an impact on climate. Potential examples of such activity include subsonic and supersonic aircraft flights that add moisture to the atmosphere at high altitude, atmospheric particles that serve as condensation nuclei, and attempts at weather modification. Man-made changes in the earth's surface can affect the albedo and the availability of solar energy. Examples of such changesinclude deforestation, erosion, extension of arid or desert land, irrigation, urbanization, and the creation of artificial lakes. Although large local climatic effects result from these activities, the global consequences are not well understood and may be insignificant.

The combustion of fuels and the use of energy result in the liberation of heat. In large, temperate-latitude cities during winter this man-made-energy can often equal or exceed that naturally available from solar radiation. Man-made energy is, however, not yet significant on a global scale but within 30 to 40 years it will equal several percent of the available solar energy over large, highly industrialized regions. The specific regional climatic consequences are unknown but are likely to be significant. Plans to build commercial fleets of supersonic aircraft that cruise in the lower stratosphere have caused some scientists, but certainly not all, to become concerned about possible stratospheric contamination. The exhaust products from these aircraft-soot particles, water vapour, nitric oxide, etc.-could attenuate solar radiation, increase cloudiness or decrease ozone concentrations. Since these substances would have a much longer average lifetime than those emitted near the earth's surface, a relatively small stratospheric emission rate could lead to significant ambient concentrations. Thus an early programme is needed to obtain baseline measurements of substances in the stratosphere and to determine whether they have a natural or man-made origin.

2. Potentially Adverse Changes on Biota and Man from Contamination by Toxic Substances including Radionuclides

This is one of the most complex and widespread of the environmental problems because many potential contaminants are involved, with the list growing each year, and immense number of species that could be affected. Many cases of local catastrophes or widespread poisoning in man and wildlife have already occurred.

The more hazardous toxic substances include heavy metals (lead, mercury and cadmium), organochlorine compounds (DDT, its degradation products and metabolites, polychlorinated biphenyls) and possibly petroleum products. Contamination occurs in all media: air, land, water and biota. Of particular importance, however, are those parts of the biosphere where the substances show long residence times, namely in soils and sea water. The sea is the ultimate repository of almost every kind of pollutant material created by man. Industrial effluents and biocides are discharged directly into coastal waters or carried to the sea by rivers. Toxic materials are often dumped in quantity on the seabed or into the open waters of the oceans. Hazardous cargoes, transported by ships as freight or fuel, are released either by accident or design into the sea. Pollutants transported by the atmosphere are continuously transferred by precipitation or direct diffusion onto the surface waters. The use of the biosphere as a recipient for toxic and other waste products will inevitably affect animal and plant species, their growth and reproduction. Every kind of pollutant in some measure affects the character of an ecosystem structure by decreasing the species diversity. Toxic substances may endanger man's health directly or by passage and accumulation through food chains. The effects of contaminants on biota can be studied by considering various biological effects, such as changes in the numbers and distribution ranges of organisms, changes in the structure of plant and animal communities, replacements of whole ecosystems and changes in productivity. Thus, by assessing selected parameters which describe changes in single species or biological systems of higher order, both specific and general effects on biota can be determined. Important changes in many species populations, including extinctions, are well known. Inadvertant or deliberate simplifications of ecosystems with a resulting decrease in stability and tolerance of environmental stress have occurred many times. The transfer of natural ecosystems to monocultural agricultural systems constitute the best examples of ecosystem simplification which now need continuous management to preserve the desired state. In some cases whole ecosystems have been completely replaced by new ones because of intensive pollution or grazing by domestic animals. Possible adverse effects on agricultural productivity are of special concern because any factor that tends to decrease the production of food and fibre must receive a high priority in the monitoring system. To arrive at the optimal combination of exploitation and management of natural resources, programmes must be developed that provide continuous information on the use of these resources and permit evaluation of the consequences of predicted future developments.

In contrast to the above problems, monitoring of radioactive contaminants is currently being efficiently provided by UNSCEAR, IAEA and other agencies. Thus, it is not anticipated that any new programmes, other than support of the current effort, will be necessary for this very important problem. In the future, however, the predicted growth of nuclear-powered electrical generatingplants will necessitate greater awarenessof the potential hazards from storage of radioactive wastes.

3. Potentially Adverse Changes in Biological Productivity Caused by Improper Land-use

The land surface in extensive parts of the world is changing because of the intense agricultural methods necessary to provide for a growing population with an increasing per capita consumption. In many parts of the world, improper land use has resulted in irreversible degradation of soils and vegetation. Soil erosion by wind and water, leaching of nutrients, salinization and extension of arid zones have been caused by such improper land-uses as overgrazing in arid zones, deforestation in areas with unstable soils and over-useof both surface and ground-water resources. Usually, these problems are local or regional in nature and are the responsibility of individual governments. However, because similar changes in soil fertility have occurred throughout the world in many nations, a global, multi-governmental approach to the problem is appropriate. Moreover, because the local effects of decreased soil fertility may be very significant, the economy of adjacent regions may also be affected. Extension of arid zones can also induce large-scale climatic changes by allowing considerable amounts of windblown dust to become airborne.

4. Potentially Adverse Changes in the Growth, Structure and Distribution of the Human Population

The fast growth of the human population in combination with changes in its distribution pattern, particularly the strong and increasing tendency towards urbanization, constitutes one of two major factors responsible for the creation of environmental problems; the other being technological developments. Among the variety of environmental problems that are affected by population growth and urbanization are: over-utilization of land; deterioration of natural areas; ecological changes; depletion of natural resources; dietary deterioration; increase of urban pathology; increased wastes; and the consequences of national policies to reduce or increase fertility.

We are satisfied that the United Nations will continue to improve its already valuable collection and evaluation of information on population size, vital statistics and demographic data which will provide supporting information both to the environmental monitoring system and to other international and national activities, particularly those related to human health monitoring.

5. Changes in the Subjective Human Perception of the Environment

Changes of the environment may or may not be harmful to man. However, both kinds of change may be perceived by people as annoying, dangerous or even irrelevant. This not only applies to laymen, but also to environmental scientists, planners and decision makers. Consequently the subjective perception of environmental problems constitutes an important factor in relation to environmental monitoring activities. It may serve as a kind of qualitative evaluation of the results of control management. Thus, although the Commission recognizes this environmental problem, it is not included as an operative part of the system.

6. Eutrophication of Waters

Both natural and man-made lakes have suffered from eutrophication and its secondary effects. In lakes receiving nitrogen and phosphorus compounds and other agricultural fertilizers, unprecedented blooms of algae have occurred. The algae themselves can spoil water quality and recreational conditions. When they die and decay, the oxygen demand may exceed the supply with resultant fish kills. The average oxygen content of some fresh water bodies has decreased very markedly in historic times. The effects of added nutrients on marine life are not well known but there may be particularly important synergistic effects, for example, if the oxidation of oil in the sea is biologically controlled. Fertilization of the seas may enhance the production of directly economically valuable species. Because eutrophication is primarily a local problem, it has not been included in the global environmental monitoring system.

7. Decreasing Freshwater Resources

The availability to man of freshwater of high quality is becoming an acute problem in many countries. Water requirements continue to increase with the growth of populations and living standards and the expansion of agriculture and industry. Water is needed for power generation irrigation, navigation and community water supply. Often it is drawn from international rivers or lakes and in many instances international co-operation is needed in the allocation of water and the financing and technical aspects of water resource development projects. The availability of ground water is most often a local problem but it has international implications in relation to the general effects which a depletion of ground water may have within a larger region.

8. Natural Disasters

Although natural disasters constitute a very important environmental problem, it is not pertinent to include a programme directly related to natural disaster monitoring or warning within the global environmental monitoring system. It is appropriate, however, that the system should provide assistance in reporting phenomena that relate to natural disasters.

Key International Efforts for Environmental protection

1. The United Nations Framework Convention on Climate Change, UNFCCC
In June 1992, the "United Nations Framework Convention on Climate Change" (UNFCCC) was signed in Rio de Janeiro by over 150 nations. The climate convention is the base for international co-operation within the climate change area. In the convention the climate problem's seriousness is stressed. There is a concern that human activities are enhancing the natural greenhouse effect, which can have serious consequences on human settlements and ecosystems.

The convention's overall objective is the stabilisation of greenhouse gas concentrations in the atmosphere at a level that would prevent dangerous anthropogenic interference with the climate system."

The principle commitment applying to parties of the convention is the adoption of policies and measures on the mitigation of climate change, by limiting anthropogenic emissions of greenhouse gases and protecting and enhancing greenhouse gas sinks and reservoirs. The commitment includes the preparation and communication of national inventories of greenhouse gases. The Climate convention does not have any quantitative targets or timetables for individual nations. However, the overall objective can be interpreted as stabilization of emissions of greenhouse gases by year 2000 at 1990 levels.

The deciding body of the climate convention is the Conference of Parties (COP). At the COP meetings, obligations made by the parties are examined and the objectives and implementation of the climate convention are further defined and developed. The first COP was held in Berlin, Germany in 1995 and the latest (COP 10) was held in December 2004, Buenos Aires, Argentina.

2. The Kyoto Protocol
There is a scientific consensus that human activities are causing global warming that could result in significant impacts such as sea level rise, changes in weather patterns and adverse health effects.

As it became apparent that major nations such as the United States and Japan would not meet the voluntary stabilization target by 2000, Parties to the Convention decided in 1995 to enter into negotiations on a protocol to establish legally binding limitations or reductions in greenhouse gas emissions. It was decided by the Parties that this round of negotiations would establish limitations only for the developed countries, including the former Communist countries (called annex A countries).

Negotiations on the Kyoto Protocol to the United Nations Framework Convention on Climate Change (UNFCCC) were completed December 11, 1997, committing the industrialized nations to specify, legally binding reductions in emissions of six greenhouse gases. The 6 major greenhouse gases covered by the protocol are carbon dioxide (CO_2), methane (CH_4), nitrous oxide (N_2O), hydrofluorocarbons (HFCs), perfluorocarbons (PFCs), and sulfur xafluoride (SF_6).

Emissions Reductions

The United States would be obligated under the Protocol to a cumulative reduction in its greenhouse gas emissions of 7% below 1990 levels for three greenhouse gases (including carbon dioxide), and below 1995 levels for the three man-made gases, averaged over the commitment period 2008 to 2012.

The Protocol states that developed countries are committed, individually or jointly, to ensuring that their aggregate anthropogenic carbon dioxide equivalent emissions of greenhouse gases do not exceed amounts assigned to each country with a view to reducing their overall emissions of such gases by at least 5% below 1990 levels in the commitment period 2008 to 2012.

The amounts for each country are listed as percentages of the base year, 1990 and range from 92% (a reduction of 8%) for most European countries--to 110% (an increase of 10%) for Iceland.

Developing Country Responsibilities

Another problematic area is that the treaty is ambiguous regarding the extent to which developing nations will participate in the effort to limit global emissions. The original 1992 climate treaty made it clear that, while the developed nations most responsible for the current buildup of greenhouse gases in the atmosphere should take the lead in combating climate change, developing nations also have a role to play in protecting the global climate. Per Capita CO_2 emissions are small in developing countries and developed nations have altered the atmosphere the most.

Developing countries, including India and China, do not have to commit to reductions in this first time period because their per-capita emissions are much lower than those of developed countries, and their economies are less able to absorb the initial costs of changing to cleaner fuels. They have not contributed significantly to today's levels of pollution that has been the product of the developed world's Industrial Revolution. The idea is that developing countries will be brought more actively into the agreement as new energy technologies develops and as they industrialize further.

Annex I and Annex II Parties

Annex I parties are countries which have commitments according to the Kyoto protocol. The entire Annex I parties are listed in the Table 9.1 below. Further Annex I parties shown in bold are also called Annex II parties. These Annex II parties have a special obligation to provide "new and additional financial sources" to developing countries (non Annex I) to help them tackle climate change, as well as to facilitate the transfer of climate friendly technologies to both developing countries and to economies in transition. Commitments are presented as percentage of base year emission levels to be achieved during between 2008 – 2012.

Table 9.1 Annex I and Annex II Parties			
European Union	%	**Economies in transition to a market economy**	%
Austria	92	Bulgaria	92
Belgium	92	Croatia	95
Denmark	92	Czech Republic	92
Finland	92	Estonia	92
France	92	Hungary	94
Germany	92	Latvia	92
Greece	92	Lithuania	92
Ireland	92	Poland	94
Italy	92	Romania	92
Luxembourg	92	Russian Federation	100
Netherlands	92	Slovakia	92
Portugal	92	Slovenia	92
Spain	92	Ukraine	100

Sweden	92
United Kingdom	92

Other Europe		Other Annex I	
Iceland	110	**Australia**	108
Liechtenstein	92	**Canada**	94
Monaco	92	**Japan**	94
Norway	101	**New Zealand**	100
Switzerland	92	**United States of America**	93

Base year is 1990 for all countries except those economies in transition, which may chose an alternative base year or multi-year period.

Actions required from developed and developing Nations

The Kyoto Protocol does call on all Parties (developed and developing) to take a number of steps to formulate national and regional programs to improve "local emission factors," activity data, models, and national inventories of greenhouse gas emissions and sinks that remove these gases from the atmosphere. All Parties are also committed to formulate, publish, and update climate change mitigation and adaptation measures, and to cooperate in promotion and transfer of environmentally sound technologies and in scientific and technical research on the climate system.

Who is bound by the Kyoto Protocol?

The Kyoto Protocol has to be signed and ratified by 55 countries (including those responsible for at least 55% of the developed world's 1990 carbon dioxide emissions) before it can enter into force. Now that Russia has ratified, this been achieved and the Protocol will enter into force on 16 February 2005.

India's Greenhouse Gas Emissions

India has experienced a dramatic growth in fossil fuel CO_2 emissions, and the data compiled by various agencies shows an increase of nearly 5.9 % since 1950. At present India is rated as the 6th largest contributor of CO_2 emissions behind China, the 2nd largest contributor. However, our per capita CO_2 of 0.93 tons per annum is well below the world average of 3.87 tons per annum. Fossil fuel emissions in India continue to result largely from coal burning. India is highly vulnerable to climate change as its economy is heavily reliant on climate sensitive sectors like agriculture and forestry. The vast low-lying and densely populated coastline is susceptible to rise in sea level.

The energy sector is the largest contributor of carbon dioxide emissions in India. The national inventory of greenhouse gases indicates that 55% of the total national emissions come from energy sector. These include emissions from road transport, burning of traditional bio-mass fuels, coal mining, and fugitive emissions from oil and natural gas.

Agriculture sector constitutes the next major contributor, accounting for nearly 34%. The emissions under this sector include those from enteric fermentation in domestic animals, manure management, rice cultivation, and burning of agriculture residues. Emissions from Industrial sector mainly came from cement production.

Indian Response to Climatic Change
Under the UNFCCC, developing countries such as India do not have binding GHG mitigation commitments in recognition of their small contribution to the greenhouse problem as well as low financial and technical capacities. The Ministry of Environment and Forests is the nodal agency for climate change issues in India. It has constituted Working Groups on the UNFCCC and Kyoto Protocol. Work is currently in progress on India's initial National Communication (NATCOM) to the UNFCCC. India ratified the Kyoto Protocol in 2002 .

The Conference of the Parties (COP)
The Conference of the Parties is the supreme body of the Climate Change Convention. The vast majority of the world's countries are members (185 as of July 2001). The Convention enters into force for a country 90 days after that country ratifies it. The COP held its first session in 1995 and will continue to meet annually unless decided otherwise. However, various subsidiary bodies that advise and support the COP meet more frequently.

The Convention states that the COP must periodically examine the obligations of the Parties and the institutional arrangements under the Convention. It should do this in light of the

Convention's objective, the experience gained in its implementation, and the current state of scientific knowledge.

Exchange of Information
The COP assesses information about policies and emissions that the Parties share with each other through their national communications. It also promotes and guides the development and periodic refinement of comparable methodologies, which are needed for quantifying net greenhouse gas emissions and evaluating the effectiveness of measures to limit them. Based on the information available, the COP assesses the Parties efforts to meet their treaty commitments and adopts and publishes regular reports on the Convention's implementation.

Support for Developing countries
Developing countries need support so that they can submit their national communications, adapt to the adverse effects of climate change, and obtain environmentally sound technologies. The COP therefore oversees the provision of new and additional resources by developed countries.

The third session of the Conference of the Parties adopted the Kyoto Protocol.

The Flexible Mechanisms
The Kyoto protocol gives the Annex I countries the option to fulfill a part of their commitments through three "flexible mechanisms". Through these mechanisms, a country can fulfill a part of their emissions reductions in another country or buy emission allowances from another country. There are three flexible mechanisms:

      i. Emissions trading
      ii. Joint implementation
      iii. Clean development mechanism

i) Emissions trading
Article 17 of the Kyoto protocol opens up for emissions trading between countries that have made commitments to reduce greenhouse gas emissions. The countries have the option to delegate this right of emissions trading to companies or other organisations.

In a system for emissions trading, the total amount of emissions permitted is pre-defined. The corresponding emissions allowances are then issued to the emitting installations through auction or issued freely. Through trading, installations with low costs for reductions are stimulated to make reductions and sell their surplus of emissions allowances to organisations where reductions are more expensive. Both the selling and buying company wins on this flexibility that trade offers with positive effects on economy, resource efficiency and climate. The environmental advantage is that one knows, in advance, the amount of greenhouse gases that will be emitted. The economical advantage is that the reductions are done where the reduction costs are the lowest. The system allows for a cost effective way to reach a pre-defined target and stimulates environmental technology development.

ii) Joint Implementation, JI

Under article 6 of the Kyoto protocol an Annex I country that has made a commitment for reducing greenhouse gases, can offer to, or obtain from another Annex I country greenhouse gas emissions reductions. These emissions reductions shall come from projects with the objectives to reduce anthropogenic emissions from sources or increase the anthropogenic uptake in sinks. In order to be accepted as JI-projects, the projects have to be accepted by both parties in advance. It also has to be proven that the projects will lead to emissions reductions that are higher than what otherwise would have been obtained. JI-projects are an instrument for one industrial country to invest in another industrial country and in return obtain emissions reductions. These reductions can be used to help fulfill their own reduction commitments at a lower cost than if they had to do the reductions in their own country.

iii) Clean Development Mechanism (CDM)

Article 12 of the Kyoto protocol defines the Clean Development Mechanism, CDM. The purpose of CDM is to:
a) contribute to sustainable development in developing countries;
b) help Annex I-countries under the Kyoto Protocol to meet their target.

With the help of CDM, countries which have set themselves an emission reduction target under the Kyoto Protocol (Annex I countries) can contribute to the financing of projects in developing countries (non-Annex I countries) which do not have a reduction target. These projects should reduce the emission of greenhouse gases while contributing to the sustainable development of the host country involved. The achieved emission reductions can be purchased by the Annex I country in order to meet its reduction target.

In order to be accepted as CDM-projects, the projects have to be accepted by both parties in advance. It also has to be proven that the projects will lead to emissions reductions that are higher than what otherwise would have been obtained. The difference between JI-projects and CDM-projects is that JI-projects are done between countries that both have commitments, while the CDM-projects is between one country that has commitments and another country that does not have commitments. Emissions reductions that have been done through CDM-projects during the period 2000 to 2007, can be used for fulfilling commitments in Annex I countries for the period 2008-2012.

How CDM works?

An investor from a developed country, can invest in, or provide finance for a project in a developing country that reduces greenhouse gas emissions so that they are lower than they would have been without the extra investment – i.e. compared to what would have happened without the CDM under a business as usual outcome. The investor then gets credits – carbon credits - for the reductions and can use those credits to meet their Kyoto target. If the CDM works perfectly it will not result in more or less emission reductions being achieved than were agreed under the Kyoto Protocol, it will simply change the location in which some of the reductions will happen.

For example, a French company needs to reduce its emissions as part of its contribution to meeting France's emission reduction target under the Kyoto Protocol. Instead of reducing emissions from its own activities in France, the company provides funding for the construction of a new biomass plant in India that would not have been able to go ahead without this investment. This, they argue, prevents the construction of new fossil-fueled plants in India, or displaces consumption of electricity from existing o reduction in greenhouse gas emissions in India. The French investor gets credit for those reductions and can use them to help meet their reduction target in France.

Requirements for Participating in CDM

Criteria	Eligible Projects
All Annex I and non-Annex I nations must meet three requirements for participation in CDM.	The CDM can include projects the following projects
• Voluntary participation	• End-use energy efficiency improvements
• Establishment of National CDM Authority	• Supply-side energy efficiency improvement
• Ratification of Kyoto Protocol	• Renewable energy
In addition Annex I nations must establish	• Fuel switching
• the assigned amount under Article 3 of the Protocol	• Agriculture (reduction of CH_4 and N_2o emissions)
• a national system for the estimation of GHG	• Industrial processes (CO_2 from cement etc., HFCs, PFCs, SF6
• a national registry	• Sinks projects (only afforestation and reforestation)
• an annual inventory and	*Note: Annex I nations must refrain from using CERs*
• an accounting system for the sale and purchase of emission reductions	*generated through nuclear energy to meet their targets*

Project cycle for CDM

The project cycle for CDM is shown in Figure 9.7. There are seven basic stages; the first four stages are performed prior to the implementation of the project, while the last three stages are performed during the lifetime of the project.

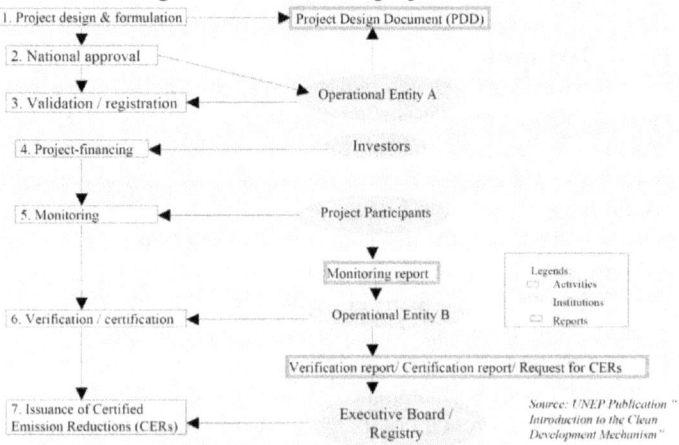

Figure: Project Cycle for CDM

While investors profit from CDM projects by obtaining reductions at costs lower than in their own countries, the gains to the developing country host parties are in the form of finance, technology, and sustainable development benefits.

Projects starting in the year 2000 are eligible to earn Certified Emission Reductions (CERs) if they lead to "real, measurable, and long-term" GHG reductions, which are additional to any that would occur in the absence of the CDM project. This includes afforestation and reforestation projects, which lead to the sequestration of carbon dioxide.

At COP-7, it was decided that the following types of projects would qualify for fast-track approval procedures:

- Renewable energy projects with output capacity up to 15 MW
- Energy efficiency improvement projects which reduce energy consumption on the supply and/or demand side by up to 15 GWh annually
- Other project activities that both reduce emissions by sources and directly emit less than 15 kilotons CO_2 equivalent annually.

The CDM will be supervised by an executive board, and a share of the proceeds from project activities will be used to assist developing countries in meeting the costs of adaptation to climate change.

Indian Initiatives on CDM

Government of India has been willing to fulfill its responsibility under the CDM. It has developed an interim criterion for approval of CDM project activities, which is now available to stakeholders. It has undertaken various capacity building activities like holding of workshops, initiation of various studies, and briefing meeting with the stakeholders. India has been actively participating in the CDM regime and has already approved projects for further development.

Under CDM, projects such as energy efficient hydrocarbon refrigerators, modernization of small scale foundry units and renovation, modernization of thermal power stations etc. are being taken up.

Case Example

In a power plant renovation and modernization programme by replacing plant equipment which are prone to wear and tear over a period of time, such as boilers and auxiliaries, turbine blades, HP governor valves and station auxiliaries which include material handling equipment, water treatment, pulverisers, ash handling plant, ESP etc resulted in CO2 emission reduction from 1.20 kg/kWh to 1.11 kg/kWh. The details are shown in the Table 9.2:

Table 9.2 Efficiency Improvement And Emission Reduction in a Power Plant Modernisation Programme

Parameters	Before the programme	After the programme
Gross heat rate (kcal/KWh)	2700	2500
Net efficiency (%)	28	30
Specific coal consumption	0.77	0.71
Total CO_2 emissions (tones/year)	1435336	1329015
CO_2 emissions (kg/ kWh)	1.20	1.11

Prototype Carbon Fund (PCF)

Recognizing that global warming will have the most impact on its borrowing client countries, the World Bank approved the establishment of the Prototype Carbon Fund (PCF). The PCF is intended to invest in projects that will produce high quality greenhouse gas emission reductions that could be registered with the United Nations Framework Convention on Climate Change (UNFCCC) for the purposes of the Kyoto Protocol. To increase the likelihood that the reductions will be recognized by the Parties to the UNFCCC, independent experts will follow validation, verification and certification procedures that respond to UNFCCC rules as they develop.

The PCF will pilot production of emission reductions within the framework of Joint Implementation (JI) and the Clean Development Mechanism (CDM). The PCF will invest contributions made by companies and governments in projects designed to produce emission reductions fully consistent with the Kyoto Protocol and the emerging framework for JI and the CDM. Contributors, or "Participants" in the PCF, will receive a pro rata share of the emission reductions, verified and certified in accordance with agreements reached with the respective countries "hosting" the projects.

Size of Market for Emissions Reductions

• All estimates of market volume are speculative at this early stage in the market's development.

• One way of looking at the potential size of the market is to assume that about one billion tonnes of carbon emissions must be reduced per year during the commitment period of 2008-2012 in order for the industrialized countries to meet their obligations of a 5% reduction in their 1990 levels of emissions.

Under Prototype carbon fund programme of the World Bank. Government of India has approved a municipal solid waste energy project for implementation in Chennai, which proposes to use the state of art technology for extracting energy from any solid waste irrespective of the energy content. Many industrial organisations in the private sector have also sought assistance under this fund.

2007 United Nations Climate Change Conference
The 2007 United Nations Climate Change Conference took place at the Bali International Conference Centre, Nusa Dua, in Bali,Indonesia, between December 3 and December 15, 2007 (though originally planned to end on 14 December). Representatives from over 180 countries attended, together with observers from intergovernmental and nongovernmental organizations. The conference encompassed meetings of several bodies, including the 13th Conference of the Parties to the United Nations Framework Convention on Climate Change (COP 13), the 3rd Meeting of the Parties to the Kyoto Protocol (MOP 3 or CMP 3), together with other subsidiary bodies and a meeting of ministers.

Negotiations on a successor to the Kyoto Protocol dominated the conference. A meeting of environment ministers and experts held in June called on the conference to agree on a road-map, timetable and 'concrete steps for the negotiations' with a view to reaching an agreement by 2009. It has been debated whether this global meeting on climate change has achieved anything significant at all.

Initial EU proposals called for global emissions to peak in 10 to 15 years and decline "well below half" of the 2000 level by 2050 for developing countries and for developed countries to achieve emissions levels 20-40% below 1990 levels by 2020. The United States strongly opposed these numbers, at times backed by Japan, Canada, Australia and Russia. The resulting compromise mandates "deep cuts in global emissions" with references to the IPCC's Fourth Assessment Report.

2014 United Nations Climate Change Conference
Aiming to raise political momentum for a global climate agreement at next year's talks in Paris in 2015 and push nations

forward in their efforts to tackle climate change, the Summit saw a record number of world leaders attend, including 100 heads of state and governmentand over 800 business, finance and civil society leaders.

Many impressive announcements were made and new coalitions launched, with leaders committing to limiting global temperature rise to less than 2 degrees Celsius and agreeing a global climate deal in Paris.

Other key outcomes include:

- 73 national governments, 11 regional governments and more than 1,000 businesses and investors showed support for pricing carbon. Together, these leaders represent 52% of global GDP, 54% of global greenhouse gas emissions and almost half of the world's population.
- EU countries pledged to reduce emissions to 40% below 1990 levels by 2030.
- A large-scale commitment to double the rate of global energy efficiency by 2030 by improvements to vehicle fuel efficiency, lighting, appliances, buildings and district energy was launched.
- The insurance industry promised to double low carbon investments to US$84 billion by the end of 2015.
- A new coalition of leaders will mobilize over US$200 billion for financing low carbon and climate-resilient development.

Examples of corporate and sub-national government commitments:

- 1,000 businesses and investors signalled their support for pricing carbon in a declaration published by the World Bank.
- A coalition of institutional investors committed to decarbonizing US$100 billion by December 2015 and tomeasure and disclose the carbon footprint of at least US$500 billion in investments.
- 10 multinationals committed to 100% renewable power, as part of a new campaign initiated by The Climate Group to help companies on their journey to becoming 100% renewable.
- A new Global Mayors Compact, representing over 2,000 cities pledged new commitments on climate action supported by new funding from public and private sources.
- A new Compact of States and Regions, co-convened by The Climate Group, committed to provide an annual account of the

climate commitments made by state and regional governments around the world and report their progress.

Environment (Protection) Act, 1986: Salient Features.

The Act came into force on Nov. 19, 1986, the birth anniversary of our Late Prime Minister Indira Gandhi, who was a pioneer of environmental protection issues in our country. The Act extends to whole of India.

Some terms related to environment have been described as follows in the Act:

(i) Environment includes water, air and land and the inter-relationships that exist among and between them and human beings, all other living organisms and property.

(ii) Environmental pollution means the presence of any solid, liquid or gaseous substance present in such concentration, as may be, or tend to be, injurious to environment.

(iii) Hazardous substance means any substance or preparation, which by its physio-chemical properties or handling is liable to cause harm to human beings, other living organisms, property or environment.

The Act has given powers to the Central Government to take measures to protect and improve environment while the state government coordinates the actions. The most important functions of Central Govt, under this Act include setting up of:

(a) The standards of quality of air, water or soil for various areas and purpose.

(b) The maximum permissible limits of concentration of various environmental pollutants (including noise) for different areas.

(c) The procedures and safeguards for the handling of hazardous substances in different areas.

(d) The prohibition and restriction on the location of industries and to carry on process and operations in different areas.

(e) The procedures and safeguards for the prevention of accidents which may cause environmental pollution and provide remedial measures for such accidents.

The power of entry and inspection, power to take sample etc. under the act lies with the Central Government or any officer empowered by it.

For the purpose of protecting and improving the quality of the environment and preventing and abating pollution, standards have been specified under Schedule- I-VI of Environment (Protection)

Rules, 1986 for emission of gaseous pollutants and discharge of effluents/waste water from industries.

These standards vary from industry to industry and also vary with the medium into which the effluent is discharged or the area of emission, for instance, the maximum permissible limits of B.O.D. (Biochemical Oxygen Demand) of the waste water is 30 ppm if it is discharged into inland waters, 350 ppm if discharged into' a public and 100 ppm, if discharged on to land or coastal region. Likewise emission standards vary in residential, sensitive and industrial area.

Under the Environmental (Protection) Rules 1986 the State Pollution Boards have to follow the guidelines provided under Schedule VI, some of which are as follows:

(a) The have to advise the Industries for treating the waste water and gases with the best available technology to achieve the prescribed standards.

(b) The industries have to be encouraged for recycling and reusing the wastes.

(c) They have to encourage the industries for recovery of biogas, energy and reusable materials.

(d) While permitting the discharge of effluents and emissions into the environment, the State Boards have to take into account the assimilative capacity of the water body.

(e) The Central and State Boards have to emphasize on the implementation of clean technologies by the industries in order to increase fuel efficiency and reduce the generation of environmental pollutants.

Under the Environment (Protection) Rules, 1986 the Central Government also made Hazardous Wastes (Management and handling) Rules 1989. Under these rules it is the responsibilities of the occupier that such wastes are properly handled and disposed off without any adverse effects.

There are 18 Hazardous Waste categories recognized under this rule and there are guidelines for their proper handling, storage, treatment, transport and disposal which should be strictly followed by the owner.

The Environment (Protection) Act, 1986 has also made provision for environmental Audit as a means of checking whether or not a company is complying with the environmental laws and regulations.

2. HAZARDOUS WASTES RULES
(MANAGEMENT, HANDLING AND TRANSPORTATION), 2008

The draft rules, namely, the Hazardous Material (Management, Handling and Trans boundary
Movement) Rules 2007 was published by the Government of India in the Ministry of Environment and Forest vide number S.O.1676(E), dated 28th September, 2007 in the Gazette of India.

Application:- These rules shall apply to the handling of hazardous wastes as specified in Schedules and shall not apply to-
(a) waste-water and exhaust gases as covered under the provisions of the Water (Prevention and Control of Pollution) Act, 1974 (6 of 1974) and the Air (Prevention and Control of Pollution) Act, 1981 (14 of 1981) and the rules made there under.
(b) wastes arising out of the operation from ships beyond five kilometres of the relevant baseline as covered under the provisions of the Merchant Shipping Act, 1958 (44 of 1958) and the rules made there under.
(c) radio-active wastes as covered under the provisions of the Atomic Energy Act, 1962 (33 of 1962) and the rules made there under.
(d) bio-medical wastes covered under the Bio-Medical Wastes (Management and Handling) Rules, 1998 made under the Act.
(e) wastes covered under the Municipal Solid Wastes (Management and Handling) Rules, 2000 made under the Act.

PROCEDURE FOR HANDLING HAZARDOUS WASTES
4. Responsibilities of the occupier for handling of hazardous wastes.-
(1) The occupier shall be responsible for safe and environmentally sound handling of hazardous wastes generated in his establishment.
(2) The hazardous wastes generated in the establishment of an occupier shall be sent or sold to a recycler or re-processor or re-user registered or authorized under these rules or shall be disposed of in an authorized disposal facility.
(3) The hazardous wastes transported from an occupier's establishment to a recycler for recycling or reuse or reprocessing

or to an authorized facility for disposal shall be transported in accordance with the provisions of these rules.

(4) The occupier or any other person acting on his behalf who intends to get his hazardous wastes treated and disposed of by the operator of a Treatment, Storage and Disposal Facility shall give to the operator of a facility, such information as may be determined by the State Pollution Control Board.

(5) The occupier shall take all adequate steps while handling hazardous wastes to:

(i) Contain contaminants and prevent accidents and limit their consequences on human beings and the environment; and

(ii) Provide persons working on the site with the training, equipment and the information necessary to ensure their safety.

5. Grant of authorization for handling hazardous wastes.

(1) Every person who is engaged in generation, processing, treatment, package, storage, transportation,use, collection, destruction, conversion, offering for sale, transfer or the like of the hazardous waste shall require to obtain an authorization from the State Pollution Control Board.

(2) The hazardous waste shall be collected, treated, re-cycled, re-processed, stored or disposed of only in such facilities as may be authorized by the State Pollution Control Board for the purpose.

(3) Every person engaged in generation, processing, treatment, package, storage, transportation, use, collection, destruction, conversion, offering for sale, transfer or the like of the hazardous waste or occupier of the facility shall make an application in **Form 1** to the State Pollution Control Board for authorization within a period of sixty days from the date of commencement of these rules: Provided that any person authorized under the provisions of the Hazardous Waste (Management and Handling) Rules, 1989, prior to the date of coming into force of these rules, shall not require to make an application for authorization till the period of expiry of such authorization.

(4) On receipt of the application complete in all respects for the authorization, the State Pollution Control Board may, after such inquiry as it considers necessary and on being satisfied that the applicant possesses appropriate facilities, technical capabilities and equipment to handle hazardous waste safely, grant within a period of one hundred and twenty days an authorization in **Form 2** to the applicant which shall be valid for a period of five years

and shall be subject to such conditions as may be laid down therein.

(5) The State Pollution Control Board may after giving reasonable opportunity of being heard to the applicant refuse to grant any authorization.

(6) Every person authorized under these rules shall maintain the record of hazardous wastes handled by him in **Form 3** and prepare and submit to the State Pollution Control Board, an annual return containing the details specified in **Form 4** on or before the 30th day of June following to the financial year to which that return relates.

(7) An application for the renewal of an authorization shall be made in **Form 1**, before its expiry and the State Pollution Control Board may renew the authorization after examining each case on merit subject to the condition that there has been no report of violation of the provisions of the Act or the rules made there under or conditions specified in the authorization.

(8) The occupier or operator of the facility shall take all the steps, wherever required, for reduction and prevention of the waste generated or for recycling or reuse and comply the conditions specified in the authorization.

(9) The State Pollution Control Board shall maintain a register containing particulars of the conditions imposed under these rules for management of hazardous waste, and it shall be open for inspection during office hours to any person interested or affected or a person authorized by him on his behalf.

6. Power to suspend or cancel an authorization.

(1) The State Pollution Control Board, may, if in its opinion the holder of the authorization has failed to comply with any of the conditions of the authorization or with any provisions of the Act or these rules and after giving him a reasonable opportunity of being heard and after recording reasons thereof in writing cancel or suspend the authorization issued under rule-4 for such period as it considers necessary in the public interest.

(2) Upon suspension or cancellation of the authorization the State Pollution Control Board may give directions to the person whose authorization has been suspended or cancelled for the safe storage of the hazardous wastes, and such person shall comply with such directions.

7. Storage of Hazardous Waste.

(1) The occupiers, recyclers, re-processors, re-users, and operators of facilities may store the hazardous wastes for a period not exceeding ninety days and shall maintain a record of sale, transfer, storage, recycling and reprocessing of such wastes and Crake these records available for inspection: Provided that the State Pollution Control Board may extend the said period in following cases, namely:-

(i) Small generators up to ten tonnes per annum;

(ii) Recyclers, re-processors and facility operators up to six months of their annual capacity;

(iii) Generators who do not have access to any Treatment, Storage, Disposal Facility in the concerned State; or

(iv) The waste which needs to be specifically stored for development of a process for its recycling, reuse.

PROCEDURE FOR RECYCLING, REPROCESSING OR REUSE OF HAZARDOUS WASTES

8. Procedure for grant of registration :

(1) Every person desirous of recycling or reprocessing the hazardous waste specified in Schedule-IV may make an application in **Form 5** accompanied with a copy each of the following documents for the grant or renewal of the registration:-

(a) Consent to establish granted by the State Pollution Control Board under the Water

(Prevention and Control of Pollution) Act, 1974 (25 of 1974) and the Air (Prevention and

Control of Pollution) Act, 1981 (21 of 1981);

(b) Certificate of registration issued by the District Industries Centre or any other government agency authorised in this regard;

(c) Proof of installed capacity of plant and machinery issued by the District Industries Centre or any other government agency authorised in this behalf; and

(d) In case of renewal, certificate of compliance of effluent, emission standards and treatment and disposal of hazardous wastes, as applicable, from the State Pollution Control Board or the Concerned Zonal Office of Central Pollution Control Board.

(2) The Central Pollution Control Board, on being satisfied that the applicant is utilizing environmentally sound technologies and possesses adequate technical capabilities, requisite facilities, and equipment to recycle, reprocess or reuse hazardous wastes, may

grant registration to such applicants stipulating therein necessary conditions for carrying out safe operations in the authorized place only.

(3) The Central Pollution Control Board shall dispose of the application for registration within a period of one hundred twenty days from the date of the receipt of such application complete in all respects.

(4) The registration, issued under sub-rule (2) shall be valid for a period of five years from the date of its issue, unless the operation is discontinued by the unit or the registration is suspended or cancelled by the Central Pollution Control Board.

(5) The Central Pollution Control Board may cancel or suspend the registration granted under these rules, if it has reasons to believe that the recycler or re-processor has failed to comply with any of the conditions of the registration, or with any provision of the Act or rules made there under.

(6) The Central Pollution Control Board may after giving a reasonable opportunity of being heard to the applicant, by order, refuse to grant or renew the registration.

(7) The recycler or re-processor shall maintain records of hazardous wastes purchased and processed and shall file an annual return of its activities of previous year in **Form 6** to the State Pollution Control Board, on or before the 30th day of June of every year.

9. Conditions for sale or transfer of Hazardous Wastes for recycling.-

The occupier generating the hazardous wastes specified in Schedule-IV may sell it only to the recycler having a valid registration from the Central Pollution Control Board for recycling or recovery.

10. Standards for recycling.-

The Central Government and Central Pollution Control Board may issue the guidelines for standards of performance for recycling processes from time to time.

11. Utilization of hazardous wastes.-

The utilisation of hazardous wastes as a supplementary resource or for energy recovery, or after processing shall be carried out by

the units only after obtaining approval from the Central Pollution
Control Board.

IMPORT AND EXPORT OF HAZARDOUS WASTES
**12. Import and export (trans boundary movement) of
hazardous wastes.-**
The Ministry of Environment and Forests shall be the nodal
Ministry to deal with the trans-boundary movement of the
hazardous wastes and to grant permission for transit of the
hazardous wastes through any part of India.

13. Import and export of hazardous wastes.-
(1) No import of the hazardous wastes from any country to India
for disposal shall be permitted.
(2) The import of Hazardous Waste from any country shall be
permitted only for the recycling or recovery or reuse.
(3) The export of hazardous wastes from India may be allowed to
an actual user of the wastes or operator of a disposal facility with
the Prior Informed Consent of the importing country to ensure
environmentally sound management of the hazardous waste in
question.
(4) No import or export of the hazardous wastes specified in
Schedule —VI shall be permitted.

14. Import or export of Hazardous Waste for recycling,
recovery and reuses.-
(1) The import and export of the hazardous wastes specified in
Schedule-III, shall be regulated in accordance with the conditions
laid down in the said schedule:
(2) Subject to the provisions contained in sub-rule (1), -
(i) The import or export of the Hazardous wastes specified in Part
A of Schedule-III shall require Prior Informed Consent of the
country from where it is imported or exported to, and shall require
the license from the Directorate General of foreign Trade and the
prior written permission of the Central Government;
(ii) The import of the hazardous wastes specified in Part B of
Schedule III shall not require Prior Informed Consent of the
country from where it is imported;
(iii) The import and export of the hazardous wastes not specified
in Part A and Part B of Schedule III but having the hazardous
characteristics outlined in Part C of the said Schedule shall require

the prior written permission of the Central Government, before it is imported into or exported from India, as the case may be.

15. Procedure for export of Hazardous Wastes from India.-

(1) Any person intending to export hazardous wastes specified in Schedule-III shall apply in **Form 7** and **Form 8** along with full cover insurance policy for consignment to the Central Government for the proposed transboundary movement of the hazardous wastes together with the Prior Informed Consent in writing from the importing country.

(2) On receipt of such application, the Central Government may give a 'No Objection Certificate' for the proposed export within a period of sixty days from the date of submission of the application and may impose conditions as it may consider necessary.

(3) The Central Government, shall forward a copy of the 'No Objection Certificate' granted under sub-rule (2), to the Central Pollution Control Board, the concerned State Pollution Control Board and the concerned Port and Customs authorities for ensuring compliance of the conditions, if any, of the export and to take appropriate steps for the safe handling of the waste shipment.

(4) The exporter shall ensure that no consignment is shipped before the 'No Objection Certificate' is received from the importing country.

(5) The exporter shall also ensure that the shipment is accompanied with the Movement Document in **Form 9.**

(6) The exporter shall inform the Ministry of Environment and Forest upon completion of the trans-boundary movement.

(7) The exporter of the hazardous wastes shall maintain the records of the hazardous wastes exported by him in **Form 10** and the record so maintained shall be available for inspection.

16. **Procedure for import of Hazardous Waste-**

(1) A person intending to import or transit for trans-boundary movement of hazardous wastes specified in Schedule-III shall apply in **Form 7** and **Form 8** to the Central Government of the proposed import wherever applicable, together with the Prior Informed Consent, which ever applicable and shall send a copy of the application, simultaneously, to the concerned State Pollution Control Board to enable them to send their comments and observations, if any, to the Ministry of Environment and Forests within a period of thirty days.

(2) On receipt of the application in complete, the Ministry of Environment and Forests shall examine the application considering the comments and observations, if any, received from the State Pollution Control Boards, and may grant the permission for import within a period of sixty days subject to the condition that the importer has-

(i) The environmentally sound recycling, recovery or reuse facilities;

(ii) Adequate facilities and arrangement for treatment and disposal of wastes generated; and

(iii) A valid registration from the Central Pollution Control Board and a proof of being an actual user, if required under these rules.

(3) The Ministry of Environment and Forests shall forward a copy of the permission granted under sub-rule (2) to the Central Pollution Control Board, the concerned State Pollution Control Board and the concerned Port and Customs authorities for ensuring compliance of the conditions of imports and safe handling of the hazardous waste.

(4) The Ministry of Environment and Forests shall communicate the permission to the importer.

(5) The Port and Customs authorities shall ensure that shipment is accompanied by the Movement Document in **Form 9** and the test report of analysis of the hazardous waste consignment in question, from a laboratory accredited by the exporting country.

(6) The Customs authority shall collect three randomly drawn samples of the consignment (prior to clearing the consignment as per the provisions laid down under the Customs Act, 1962) for analysis and retain the report for a period of two years, in order to ensure that in the event of any dispute, as to whether the consignment conforms or not to the declaration made in the application and Movement Document.

(7) The importer of the hazardous waste shall maintain records of the hazardous waste imported by him in **Form 10** and the record so maintained shall be available for inspection.

(8) The importer shall also inform the concerned State Pollution Control Board and the Central Pollution Control Board, the date and time of the arrival of the consignment of the hazardous waste ten days in advance.

17. **Illegal Traffic.-**

(1) The export and import of hazardous wastes from and into India shall be deemed illegal if-

(i) It is without permission of the Central Government in accordance with these rules, or

(ii) The permission has been obtained through falsification, mis-representation or fraud; or

(iii) It does not conform to the shipping details provided in the movement documents; or

(iv) It results in deliberate disposal (i.e., dumping) of hazardous wastes in contravention of the Basel Convention and of general principles of International or National Law.

(2). In case of illegal import of the hazardous wastes, the importer shall re-export the waste in question at his cost within a period of ninety days from the date of its arrival into India and its implementation will be ensured by the concerned State Pollution Control Board.

TREATMENT, STORAGE AND DISPOSAL FACILITY FOR HAZARDOUS WASTES

18. Treatment, Storage and Disposal-Facility for hazardous wastes.-

(1) The State Government, occupier, operator of a facility or any association of occupiers shall individually or jointly or severally be responsible for, and identify sites for establishing the facility for treatment, storage and disposal of the hazardous wastes in the State.

(2) The operator of common facility or occupier of a captive facility, shall design and set up the Treatment, Storage and Disposal Facility as per technical guidelines issued by the Central Pollution Control Board in this regard from time to time and shall obtain approval from the State Pollution Control Board for design and layout in this regard from time to time.

(3) The State Pollution Control Board shall monitor the setting up and operation of the Treatment, Storage and Disposal Facilities regularly.

(4) The operator of the Treatment, Storage and Disposal Facility shall be responsible for safe and environmentally sound operation of the Treatment, the Storage and Disposal Facility and its closure and post closure phase, as per guidelines issued by the Central Pollution Control Board from time to time.

(5) The operator of the Treatment, Storage and Disposal Facility shall maintain records of hazardous wastes handled by him in **Form 10.**

PACKAGING, LABELLING, AND TRANSPORT OF HAZARDOUS WASTE
19. Packaging and labeling.-
(1) The occupier or operator of the Treatment, Storage and Disposal Facility or recycler shall ensure that the hazardous waste are packaged and labelled, based on the composition in a manner suitable for safe handling, storage and transport as per the guidelines issued by the Central Pollution Control Board from time to time.

(2) The labelling and packaging shall be easily visible and be able to withstand physical conditions and climatic factors.

20. Transportation of Hazardous waste.-
(1) The transport of the hazardous wastes shall be in accordance with the provisions of these rules and the rules made by the Central Government under the Motor Vehicles Act. 1988 and other guidelines issued from time to time in this regard.

(2) The occupier shall provide the transporter with the relevant information in **Form 11**, regarding the hazardous nature of the wastes and measures to be taken in case of an emergency and shall mark the hazardous wastes containers as per **Form 12**.

(3) In case of transport of hazardous wastes for final disposal to a facility for treatment, storage and disposal existing in a State other than the State where the hazardous waste is generated, the occupier shall obtain 'No Objection Certificate' from the State Pollution Control Board of both the States.

(4) In case of transportation of hazardous wastes through a State other than the State of origin or destination, the occupier shall intimate the concerned State Pollution Control Boards before he hands over the hazardous wastes to the transporter.

21. Manifest system (Movement Document to be used within the country only).-
(1) The occupier shall prepare six copies of the manifest in **Form 13** comprising of colour code indicated below and all six copies shall be signed by the transporter:

Copy number withcolour code

Copy 1 (White) To be forwarded by the occupier to the State Pollution Control Board or
Committee.

Copy 2 (Yellow) To be carried by the occupier after taking signature on it form the transporter and the rest of the four copies to be carried by the transporter.

Copy 3 (pink) To be retained by the operator of the facility after signature.

Copy 4 (orange) To be returned to the transporter by the operator of facility/recycler after accepting waste.

Copy 5 (green) To be returned by the operator of the facility to State Pollution Control Board/Committee after treatment and disposal of wastes.

Copy 6 (blue) To be returned by the operator of the facility to the occupier after treatment and disposal of hazardous materials/wastes.

(2) The occupier shall forward copy 1 (white) to the State Pollution Control Board, and in case the hazardous wastes is likely to be transported through any transit State, the occupier shall prepare an additional copy each for intimation to such State and, forward the same to the concerned State Pollution Control Board before he hands over the hazardous wastes to the transporter.

(3) No transporter shall accept hazardous wastes from an occupier for transport unless it is accompanied by copies 3 to 6 of the manifest.

(4) The transporter shall submit copies 3 to 6 of the manifest duly signed with date to the operator of the facility along with the waste consignment.

(5) Operator of the facility upon completion of treatment and disposal operations of the hazardous wastes shall forward copy 5 (green) to the State Pollution Control Board and copy 6 (blue) to the occupier and the copy 3 (pink) shall be retained by the operator of the facility.

3. THE PUBLIC LIABILITY INSURANCE ACT, 1991

The following Act of Parliament received the assent of the President on the 22nd January, 1991, and is hereby published for general information:-

An Act to provide for public liability insurance for the purpose of providing immediate relief to the persons affected by accident occurring while handling any hazardous substance and for matters connected therewith or incidental there to.

BE it enacted by Parliament in the forty-first Year of The Republic of India as follows:-

1. SHORT TITLE AND COMMENCEMENT
(1) This Act may be called the Public Liability Insurance Act, 1991.

(2) It shall come into force on such date as the Central Government may, by notification, appoint.

2. DEFINITIONS
In this Act, unless the context otherwise requires.-

(a) **Accident**[1] means an accident involving a fortuitous, sudden or unintentional occurrence while handling any hazardous substance resulting in continuous, intermittent or repeated exposure to death, of or injury to, any person or damage to any property but does not include an accident by reason only of war or radio-activity.

(b) **Collector** means the Collector having jurisdiction over the area in which the accident occurs.

(c) **Handling**, in relation to any hazardous substance, means the manufacture, processing, treatment, package, storage, transportation by vehicle, use, collection, destruction, conversion, offering for sale, transfer or the like of such hazardous substance.

(d) **Hazardous substance** means any substance or preparation which is defined as hazardous substance under the Environment (Protection) Act, 1986 (29 of 1986), and exceeding such quantity as may be specified, by notification, by the Central Government.

(e) **Insurance** means insurance against liability under sub-section (1) of section 3:

(f) **Notification** means a notification published in the official Gazette.

(g) **Owner**[2] means a person who owns, or has control over handling any hazardous substance at the time of accident and includes,-

(i) in the case of firm, any of its partners.

(ii) in the case of an association, any of its members.

(iii) in the case or a company, any of its directors, managers, secretaries or other officers who is directly in charge of, and is responsible to the company for the conduct of the business of the Company.

(h) **Prescribed** means prescribed by rules made under this Act.

(ha) **Relief Fund**[3] means the Environmental Relief Fund establishment

under section 7A]

(i) "rules" means rules made under this Act;

(ii) "vehicle" means any mode of surface transport other than railways.

3. LIABILITY TO GIVE RELIEF IN CERTAIN CASES ON PRINCIPLE OF NO FAULT

(1) Where death or injury to any person (other than a workman) or damage to any property has resulted from an accident, the owner shall-be liable to give such relief as is specified in Schedule for such death, injury or damage.

(2) In any claim for relief under sub-section (I) (hereinafter referred to in this Act as claim for relief), the claimant shall not be required to plead and establish that the death, injury or damage in respect of which the claim has been made was due to any wrongful act, neglect or default of any person.

Explanation.-For the purpose of this section,-

(i) **Workman** has the meaning assigned to it in the Workmen's Compensation Act, 1923 (8 of 1923);

(ii) **Injury** includes permanent total or permanent partial disability or sickness resulting out of an accident.

1 Substituted by the Public Liability Insurance (Amendment) Act. 1992 dt. 31.1.92.

2 Substituted by the Public Liability Insurance (Amendment) Act. 1992, dated 31.1.1992.

3 Substituted, Ibid.

4. LIABILITY OF OWNER TO TAKE OUT INSURANCE POLICIES

(1) Every owner shall take out, before he starts handling any hazardous substance, one or more insurance policies providing for contracts of insurance thereby he is insured against liability to give relief under sub-section (1) of section 3; Provided that any owner handling any hazardous substance immediately before the commencement of this Act shall take out such insurance policy or policies as soon as may be and in any case within a period of one year from such commencement.

(2) Every owner shall get the insurance policy, referred to in subsection (1), renewed from time to time before the expiry of the period of validity thereof so that the insurance policies may remain in force throughout the period during which such handling is continued.

1(2A) No insurance policy taken out by an owner shall be for a amount less than the amount of the paid-up capital of the under taking handling any hazardous substance and owned or controlled by that owner and more than the amount, not exceeding fifty crore rupees, as may be prescribed.

Explanation.- "Paid-up capital" in this sub-section means, in the case of an owner not being a company, the market value of all assets and stocks of the undertaking on the date of contracts of insurance.

(2B) The liability of the insurer under one insurance policy shall not exceed the amount specified in the terms of the contract of insurance in that insurance policy.

(2C) Every owner shall also, together with the amount of premium, pay to the insurer, for being credited to the Relief Fund established under section 7A, such further amount, not exceeding the amount of premium, as may be prescribed.

(2D) The insurer shall remit the further amount received from the owner under sub-section (2C) to the Relief Fund in such manner and within such period as may be prescribed and where the insurer fails to so remit the further amount, such amount shall be recoverable from insurer as arrears of land revenue or of public demand.

(3)The Central Government may, by notification, exempt from the operation of sub-section (1) any owner, namely:-

(a) The Central Government;

1 Inserted by the Public Liability Insurance (Amendment) Act, 1992 dt. 31.1.1992.

(b) Any State Government,

(c) Any corporation owned or controlled by the Central Government or a State Government; or

(d) Any local authority:

Provided that no such order shall be made in relation to such owner unless a fund has been established and is maintained by that owner in accordance with the rules made in this behalf for meeting any liability under sub-section (1) of section 3.

5. VERIFICATION AND PUBLICATION OF ACCIDENT BY COLLECTOR

Whenever it comes to the notice of the Collector that an accident has occurred at any place within his jurisdiction, he shall verify the occurrence of such accident and cause publicity to be given in such manner as he deems fit for inviting applications under sub-section (1) of section 6.

6. APPLICATION FOR CLAIM FOR RELIEF

(1) An application for claim for relief may be made-

(a) By the person who has sustained the injury;

(b) By the owner of the property to which the damage has been caused;

(c) Where death has resulted from the accident, by all or any of the legal representatives of the deceased; or

(d) By any agent duly authorised by such person or owner of such property or all or any of the legal representatives of the deceased, as the case may be:

Provided that where all the legal representatives of the deceased have not joined in any such application for relief, the application shall be made on behalf of or for the benefit of all the legal representatives of the deceased and the legal representatives who have not so joined shall be impleaded as respondents to the application.

(2) Every application under sub-section (I) shall be made to the Collector and shall be in such form, contain such particulars and shall be accompanied by such documents as may be prescribed.

(3) No application for relief shall be entertained unless it is made within five years of the occurrence of the accident.

7. AWARD OF RELIEF

(1) On receipt of an application under sub-section (1) of section 6, the Collector shall after giving notice of the application to the owner and after giving the parties an opportunity of being heard, hold an inquiry into the claim or, each of he claims, and may make an award determining the amount of relief which appears to him to be just and specifying the person or persons to whom such amount of relief shall be paid.

(2) The Collector shall arrange to deliver copies of the award to the parties concerned expeditiously and in any case within a period of fifteen days from the date of the award.

1[(3) When an award is made under this section,-

(a) the insurer, who is required to pay any amount in terms of such award and to the extend specified in sub-section (2B) of section 4, shall, within a period of thirty days of the date of announcement of the award, deposit that amount in such manner as the Collector may direct;

(b) the Collector shall arrange to pay from the Relief Fund, in terms of such award and in accordance with the scheme made under section 7A, to the person or persons referred to in sub-section (1) such amount in such manner as may be specified in that scheme;

(c) the owner shall, within such period, deposit such amount in such manner as the Collector may direct.]

(4) In holding any inquiry under sub-section (1), the Collector may, subject to any rules made in this behalf, follow such summary procedure as he thinks fit.

(5) The Collector shall have all the powers of Civil Court for the purpose of taking evidence on oath and of enforcing the attendance of witnesses and of compelling the discovery and production of documents and material objects and for such other purposes as may be prescribed; and the Collector shall be deemed to be a Civil Court for all the purposes of section 195 and Chapter XXVI of the Code of Criminal Procedure, 1973 (2 of 1974).

(6) Where the insurer or the owner against whom the award is made under subsection

(1) fails to deposit the amount of such award within the period specified under sub-section (3), such amount shall be recoverable from the owner, or as the case may be, the insurer as arrears of land revenue or of public demand.

1 Substituted by the Public Liability Insurance (Amendment) Act, 1992 dt. 31.1.1992.

(7) A claim for relief in respect of death of, or injury to, any person or damage to any property shall be disposed of as expeditiously as possible and every endeavour shall be made to dispose of such claim within three months of the receipt of the application for relief under sub-section (1) of section 6.

1[(8) Where an owner is likely to remove or dispose of his property with a view to evading payment by him of the amount of award, the Collector may, in accordance with the provisions contained in rules 1 to 4 of Order XXXIX of the First Schedule to the Code of Civil Procedure, 1908, (5 of 1908), grant a temporary injunction to restrain such act.]

2[7A. ESTABLISHMENT OF ENVIRONMENTAL RELIEF FUND

(1) The Central Government may, by notification in the official Gazette, establish a fund to be known as the Environment Relief Fund.

(2) The Relief Fund shall be utilised for paying, in accordance with the provisions of this Act and the scheme, relief under the award made by the Collector under section 7.

(3) The Central Government may, by notification in the Official Gazette, make a scheme specifying the authority in which the relief fund shall vest, the manner in which the Fund shall be administered the form and the manner in which money shall be drawn from the Relief Fund and for all other matters connected with or incidental to the administration of the Relief Fund and the payment of relief therefrom.]

8. PROVISIONS AS TO OTHER RIGHT TO CLAIM COMPENSATION FOR
DEATH, ETC

(1) The right to claim relief under sub-section (1) of section 3 in respect of death of, or injury to, any person or damage to any property shall be in addition to any other right to claim compensation in respect thereof under any other law for the time being in force.

(2) Notwithstanding anything contained in sub-section (1), where in respect of death of, or injury to, any person or damage to any

1 Substituted by the Public Liability Insurance (Amendment) Act, 1992 dt. 31.1.1992.

2 Inserted by the Public Liability Insurance (Amendment) Act, 1992 dl. 31.1.92.

property, the owner, liable to give claim for relief, is also liable to pay compensation under any other law, the amount of such compensation shall be reduced by the amount of relief paid under this Act.

9. POWER TO CALL FOR INFORMATION

Any person authorised by the Central Government may, for the purposes of ascertaining whether any requirements of this Act or of any rule or of any direction given under this Act have been compiled with, require any owner to submit to that person such information as that person may reasonably think necessary.

10. POWER OF ENTRY AND INSPECTION

Any person, authorised by the Central Government in this behalf, shall have a right to enter, at all reasonable times with such assistance as he considers necessary, any place, premises or vehicle, where hazardous substance is handled for the purpose of determining whether any provisions of this Act or of any rule or of any direction given under this Act is being or has been compiled with and such owner is bound to render all assistance to such person.

11. POWER OF SEARCH AND SEIZURE

(1) If a person, authorised by the Central Government in this behalf, has reason to believe that handling of any hazardous substance is taking place in any place premises or vehicle, in contravention of sub-section (1) of section 4, he may enter into and search such place, premises or vehicle for such handling of hazardous substance.

(2) Where, as a result of any search under sub-section (1) any handling of hazardous substance has been found in relation to which contravention of sub-section (1) of section 4 has taken place, he may seize such hazardous substance and other things which, in his opinion, will be useful for, or relevant to, any proceeding under this Act:

Provided that where it is not practicable to seize any such substance or thing he may serve on the owner an order that the owner shall not remove, part with, or otherwise deal with, the hazardous substance and such other things except with the previous permission of that person.

(3) He may, if he has reason to believe that it is expedient so to do to prevent an accident dispose of the hazardous substance seized under sub-section (2) immediately in such manner as he may deem fit.

(4) All expenses incurred by him in the disposal of hazardous substances under sub-section (3) shall be recoverable from the owner as arrears of land revenue or of public demand.

12. POWER TO GIVE DIRECTIONS

Notwithstanding anything contained in any other law but subject to the provisions of this Act, the Central Government may, in exercise of its powers and performance of its functions under this Act, issue such directions in writing as it may deem fit for the purposes of this Act to any owner or any person, officer, authority or agency and such owner, person, officer, authority or agency shall be bound to comply with such directions.

Explanation.-For the removal of doubts, it is hereby declared that the power to issue directions under this section includes the power to direct-

(a) prohibition or regulation of the handling of any hazardous substance; or

(b) stoppage or regulation of the supply of electricity, water or any other service.

13. POWER TO MAKE APPLICATION TO COURTS FOR RESTRAINING OWNER FROM HANDLING HAZARDOUS SUBSTANCES

(1) If the Central Government or any person authorised by that Government in this behalf has reason to believe that any owner has been handling any hazardous substance in contravention of any of the provisions of this Act, that Government or, as the case may be, that person may make an application to a Court, not inferior to that of a Metropolitan Magistrate or a Judicial Magistrate first class for restraining such owner from such handling.

(2) On receipt of the application under sub-section (1), the Court may make such order as it deems fit.

(3) Where under sub-section (2), the Court makes an order restraining any owner from handling hazardous substance. it may. in that order-

(a) direct such owner to desist from such handling;

(b) aulhorise the Central Government or, as the case may be, the person referred to in sub-section (1), if the direction under clause (a) is not complied with by the owner to whom such direction is issued, to implement the direction in such manner as may be specified by the Court.

(4) All expenses incurred by the Central Government, or as the case may be, the person in implementing the directions of Court under clause (b) of sub-section (3), shall be recoverable from the owner as arrears of land revenue or of public demand

14. PENALTY FOR CONTRAVENTION OF SUB-SECTION (1) OR SUBSECTION (2) OF SECTION 4 OR FAILURE TO COMPLY WITH DIRECTIONS UNDER SECTION 12

(1) Whoever contravenes any of the provisions of 1[sub-section (1), sub-section

(2), sub-section (2A) or sub-section (2C)] of section 4 or fails to comply with any directions issued under section 12, he shall be punishable imprisonment for a term which shall not be less than one year and six months but which may extend to six years, or with fine which shall not be less than one lakh rupees, or with both.

(2) Whoever, having already been convicted of an offence under sub-section (1), is convicted for the second offence or any offence subsequent to the second offence, he shall be punishable with imprisonment for a term which shall not be less than two years but which may extend to seven years and with fine which shall not be less than one lakh rupees.

(3) Nothing contained in section 360 of thc Code of Criminal Procedure, 1973 (2 of 1974), or in the Probation of Offenders Act, 1958 (20 of 1958), shall apply to a person convicted of an offence under this Act unless such person is under eighteen years of age.

15. PENALTY FOR FAILURE TO COMPLY WITH DIRECTION UNDER SECTION 9 OR ORDER UNDER SECTION 11 OR OBSTRUCTING ANY PERSON IN DISCHARGE OF HIS FUNCTIONS UNDER SECTION 10 OR 11

If any owner fails to comply with direction issued under section 9 or fails to comply with order issued under sub-section (2) of section 11, or obstructs any person in discharge of his functions under section 10 or sub-section (1) or sub-section (3) of section

11, he shall be punishable with imprisonment which may extend to three months, or with fine which may extend to ten thousand rupees, or with both.

16. OFFENCES BY COMPANIES

(1) Where any offence under this Act has been committed by a company, every person who, at the time the offence was committed, was directly in charge of, and was responsible to, the company for the conduct of the business of the company, as well as the company, shall be deemed to be guilty of the offence and shall be liable to be proceeded against and punished accordingly. Provided that nothing contained in this sub-section shall render any such person liable to any punishment provided in this Act, if he proves that the offence was committed without his knowledge or that he exercised all due diligence to prevent the commission of such offence.

(2) Notwithstanding anything contained in sub-section (1), where an offence under this Act has been committed by a company and it is proved that the offence has been committed with the consent or connivance of, or is attributable to any neglect on the part of, any director, manager, secretary or other officer of the company, such director, manager, secretary or other officer shall also be deemed to be guilty of that offence and shall be liable to be proceeded against and punished accordingly.

Explanation--For the purposes of this section,--

(a) "company" means any body corporate and includes a firm or other association of individual;

(b) "director", in relation to a firm, means a partner in the firm.

17. OFFENCES BY GOVERNMENT DEPARTMENTS

Where an offence under this Act has been committed by any Department of Government, the Head of the Department shall be deemed to be guilty of the offence and shall be liable to be proceeded against and punished accordingly:

Provided that nothing contained in this section shall render such Head of the Department liable to any punishment if he proves that the offence was committed without his knowledge or that he exercised all due diligence to prevent the commission of such offence.

1 Substituted by the Public Liability Insurance (Amendment) Act, 1992 dt. 31.1.92.

18. COGNIZANCE OF OFFENCES
No court shall take cognizance of any offence under this Act except on a complaint made by-
(a) The Central Government or any authority or officer authorised in this behalf by that Government; or
(b) any person who has given notice of not less than sixty days in the manner prescribed, of the alleged offence and of his intention to make a complaint, to the Central Government or the authority or officer authorised as aforesaid.

19. POWER TO DELEGATE
The Central Government may, by notification delegate, subject to such conditions and limitations as may be specified in the notification, such of its powers and functions under this Act (except the power under section 23) as it may deem necessary or expedient to any person (including any officer, authority or other agency).

20. PROTECTION OF ACTION TAKEN IN GOOD FAITH
No suit, prosecution or other legal proceeding shall lie against the Government or the person, officer, authority or other agency in respect of anything which is done or intended to be done in good faith in pursuance of this Act or the rules made or orders or directions issued there under.

21. ADVISORY COMMITTEE
(1) The Central Government may, from time to time, constitute an Advisory Committee on the matters relating to the insurance policy under this Act.
(2) The Advisory Committee shall consist of--
(a) Three officers representing the Central Government;
(b) two persons representing the insurers;
(c) two persons representing the owners; and
(d) two persons from amongst the experts of insurance or hazardous substances, to be appointed by the Central Government.
(3) The Chairman of the Advisory Committee shall be one of the members representing the Central Government. nominated in this behalf by that Government.

22. EFFECT OF OTHER

The provisions of this Act and any rules made there under shall have effect not withstanding anything inconsistent therewith contained in any other law

23. POWER TO MAKE RULES

(1) The Central Government may, by notification, make rules for carrying out the purposes of this Act.

(2) In particular, and without prejudice to the generality of the foregoing power, such rules may provide for all or any of the following matters, namely-

1[(a) the maximum amount for which an insurance policy may be taken out by an owner under sub-section (2A) of section 4;

(aa) the amount required to be paid by every owner for being credited to the Relief Fund under sub-section (2C) of section 4;

(ab) the manner in which and the period within the amount received from the owner is required to be remitted by the insurer under sub-section (2D) of section 4];

2[(ac) establishment and maintenance of fund under sub-section (3) of section 4];

(b) the form of application and the particulars to be given therein and the documents to accompany such application under sub-section (2) of section 6;

(c) the procedure for holding an inquiry under sub-section (4) of section 7;

(d) the purposes for which the Collector shall have powers of a Civil Court under sub-section (5) of section 7;

(e) the manner in which notice of the offence and of the intention to make a complaint to the Central Government shall be given under clause (b) of section 18;

(f) any other matter which is required to be, or may be, prescribed.

3[(3) Every rule or scheme made under this Act shall be laid, as soon as may be after it is made, before each House of Parliament, while it is in session or a total period of thirty days which may be comprised in one session or in two or more successive sessions, and if, before the expiry of the session immediately following the session or the successive sessions aforesaid, both Houses agree in making any modification in the rule or scheme or both Houses agree that the rule or scheme should not be made, the rule or scheme shall thereafter have effect only in such modified form or be of no effect, as the case may be; so,. however, that any such modification or annulment shall be without prejudice to the validity of anything previously done under that rule or scheme.]

THE SCHEDULE.

[See Section 3(1)]

(i) Reimbursement of medical expenses incurred up to a maximum of Rs. 12,500 in each case.

(ii) For fatal accidents the relief will be Rs. 25,000 per person in addition to reimbursement of medical expenses if any, incurred on the victim up to a maximum of Rs. 12,500.

(iii) For permanent total or permanent partial disability or other injury or sickness, the relief will be (a) reimbursement of medical expenses incurred, if any, up to a maximum of Rs. 12,500 in each case and (b) cash relief on the basis of percentage of disablement as certified by an authorised physician. The relief for total permanent disability will be Rs. 25,000.

(iv) For loss of wages due to temporary partial disability which reduces the earning capacity of the victim, there will be a fixed monthly relief not exceeding Rs.1,000 per month up to a maximum of 3 months: provided the victim has been hospitalised for a period of exceeding 3 days and is above 16 years of age.

(v) Up to Rs. 6,000 depending on the actual damage, for any damage to private property.

1 Inserted by the Public Liability Insurance (Amendment) Act, 1992 dt. 31.1.92.
2 Re-lettered, Ibid,
3 Substituted by the Public Liability Insurance (Amendment) Act, 1992 dt. 31.1.1992.

4. WATER ACT (PREVENTION AND CONTROL OF POLLUTION) 1974

Water constitutes an important and integral part of our environment. Water is a colourless, odourless, and transparent liquid substance. These are the qualities of water but are lost when water becomes polluted and contaminated. As a result, it becomes unfit for use. In other words, although water is an important and essential element of human life, it is useful only when not contaminated and injurious to public and animal health, and aquatic life.

Salient features of the Water (Prevention and Control of Pollution) Act, 1974

1. Water (Prevention and Control of Pollution) Act, 1974 is an appropriate step for the management of water pollution; the maintenance or restoration of wholesomeness of water; the establishment, with a view to carrying out the purposes aforementioned, of Boards for the prevention and control of water pollution; conferring on and assigning to such Boards powers and functions relating thereto and for matters connected therewith.

2. The Act deals with a particular type of pollution and presents an integrated approach to tackle the problem. It is an important legislative measure which has been enacted to implement the decision taken in the United Nation's Conference on Human Environment held in June 1972 at Stockholm.

3. The Water (Prevention and Control of Pollution) Act, 1974 has 64 Sections and has been divided into eight chapters relating to i) Preliminary, ii) Central and State Boards for the Prevention and Control of Water Pollution, iii) Joint Boards, iv) Powers and Functions of Boards, v) Prevention and Control of Water Pollution, vi) Funds, Accounts and Audit, vii) Penalties and Procedures, and viii) Miscellaneous.

4. The Act provides for the creation of the Central Pollution Control Board and State Pollution Control Boards. It authorises the establishment of the Joint Boards. The main function of the Central Board, under Section 16(1) of the Act, is to promote cleanliness of streams and wells

in the States. Section 16(2) provides certain functions in the nature of advice, planning, co-ordination, publications, education and programmes for preventing, controlling and abating water pollution.

5. The State Boards (under Section 17) of the Act are expected not only to plan comprehensive programmes for the prevention and control of water pollution in the State but also to inspect sewage or trade effluents, works and plants for their treatment, to lay down standards for such effluents, their treatment and for the quality of receiving waters, and to make orders for waste disposal and the like.

6. Under the Water (Prevention and Control of Pollution) Act, 1974, power to give "directions" is conferred on-
   - The Central Government (which can give directions to the Central Boards),
   - The Central Board (which can give directions to the State Boards),
   - The State Government (which can give directions to State Boards).
   - In case of conflict between directions given by the Central Government, that matter shall be referred to the Central Government for decision. If the Central Board's directions are not complied with by the - State Board, the Central Board can order the former to perform the functions of the latter for a specified period.

7. The Act provides that the State Government in consultation with the State Board is empowered to declare any area or areas within the jurisdiction of the concerned State as "Water Pollution Prevention and Control Area".

8. Apart from the general powers of the State Boards (Section 17), a State Board has statutory powers to obtain information (Section 20), to take samples of effluents and have them analysed (Sections 21-22) and enter and inspect premises and vessels (Section 23). Violation is punishable under Section 40.

9. The Act prohibits every person from knowingly doing certain acts which cause water pollution. Most important is the prohibition against causing or permitting the entry into any stream or well or sewer or on land of-

- any poisonous matter,
- any noxious matter,
- any polluting matter a per standards laid by State Board,
- any other matter tending to impede the proper flow of water of a stream "in a manner leading or likely to lead to a substantial aggravation of pollution due to other causes or its consequences".
-Violation is punishable under Section 43 of the Act.

10. The Act prohibits the following acts, if committed without the previous consent of the State Board:
-establishment of any industry etc. or any treatment and disposal system likely to lead to discharge of sewage,
- bringing into use any new discharge or sewage, or
- beginning to make any new discharge or sewage.

11. The Act lays down the circumstances in which such consent may be granted. Orders refusing consent are, under Section 28, appealable to the prescribed appellate authority. They can also be revised by the State Government under Section 29 of the Act.

12. The Act provides for the appeal by any person aggrieved by an order made by the State Board under Section 25 (Restrictions on new outlets and new discharges), Section 26 (Provision regarding existing discharge of sewage or trade effluent), Section 27 (Refusal or withdrawal of consent by the State Board) may within thirty days from the date on which the order is communicated to him, refer an appeal to such an authority or appellate authority as the State Government may think fit to constitute.

13. The Act provides that the State Government may at any time, either of its own motion or on an application made to it in this behalf, call for the records of any case where an order has been made by the State Board under Section 25 (Restrictions on new outlets and new discharges), Section 26 (Provision regarding existing discharge of sewage or trade effluent), or Section 27 (Refusal or withdrawal of consent by the State Board) for the purpose of satisfying itself as to the legality or propriety of any such order and may pass such order in relation thereto as it may think fit after giving reasonable

opportunity of being heard in the matter to the appealing person.

14. The Act provides that where the consent of the Board is subject to the condition of execution of work and the person to whom such conditional consent is given fails to execute the works, the State Board can get those works executed at his costs.

15. The Act imposes on the person concerned, an obligation to inform the State Board where owing to any accident etc, there is any discharge of person poisonous, noxious or polluting matter. Failure to do so is punishable under Section 45a, which is the residuary penal provision.

16. By Section 32, the State Board is empowered to take emergency measures if it appears to them that any poisonous, noxious or polluting matter is present in any stream or well or on, even due to any accident or other unforeseen act or event, and if the Board is of the opinion that it is necessary to take immediate action, it may for the reasons to be recorded in writing, carry out such operations as it may consider necessary.

17. The Act provides that, where it is apprehended by a Board that the water in any stream or well is likely to be polluted by reason of the disposal or likely disposal of any matter in such stream or well or in any sewer, or on any land, or otherwise, the Board may make an application to a Court, not inferior to that of a Metropolitan Magistrate or a Judicial Magistrate of the first Class, for restraining the person who is likely to cause such pollution from so causing.

18. Under the Water (Prevention and Control of Pollution) Act, 1974 (subject to directions of the Central Government) a Board can, in the exercise of its powers and performance of its functions under the Act, issue directions. Breach of such directions is punishable under Section 41.

-The Water (Prevention and Control of Pollution) Act, 1974 is of considerable importance in practice. It provides for penalties and punishments for non-compliance of the directions given by the State Board, for certain acts and for contravention of provisions of the Act. The punishment under the Act may

- be imprisonment for a term varying from three months to seven years and / with
- a fine which may extend to ten thousand rupees, with an additional fine which may extend to five thousand rupees for every day during which such failure continues after the conviction for the first such failure.
- If the failure continues beyond a period of one year after the date of conviction, the offender shall, on conviction, be punishable with imprisonment for a term which shall not be less than two years but which may extend to seven years and with fine.

19. The Act provides for enhanced penalty if any person who has been convicted of any offence under Section 24 (Prohibition on use of stream or well for disposal of polluting matter, etc.) or Section 25 (Restrictions on new outlets and new discharges) or Section 26 (Provision regarding existing discharge of sewage or trade effluent) is again found guilty of an offence involving a contravention of the same provision, he shall, on the second and on every subsequent conviction, be punishable with imprisonment for a term which shall not be less than one and half years but which may extend to six years and with fine. No cognisance shall be taken of any conviction made more than two years before the commission of the offence which is being punished.

20. The Act provides penalty, for the contravention / failure of compliance of any order or direction given under certain provisions of this Act, for which no penalty has been elsewhere provided in this Act, of an imprisonment for a term which may extend to three months or with fine which may extend to ten thousand rupees or both and in the case of a continuing contravention or failure, with an additional fine which may extend to five thousand rupees for every day during which such contravention or failure continues after conviction for the first such contravention or failure.

21. Under the Act, when an offence under this Act has been committed by a company, every person at the time the offence was committed who was in-charge of, and was responsible to the company for the conduct of, the business of the company, as well as the company, shall

be deemed to be guilty of the offence and shall be liable to be proceeded against and punished accordingly. But the person held guilty proves that the offence was committed without his knowledge or that he exercised all due diligence to prevent the commission of such an offence, in such situation he is not liable for punishment provided under the Act. When an offence under this Act is committed by the company with the consent or connivance or commission of such offence is attributable to the neglect of any director, manager, officer, secretary or any other officer of the company, shall be liable to be proceeded against and punished accordingly.

22. When an offence under this Act has been committed by any Department of Government, the Head of the Department shall be deemed to be guilty of the offence and shall be liable to be proceeded against and punished accordingly. But if the Head of the Department proves that the offence was committed without his knowledge or that he exercised all due diligence to prevent the commission of such offence, he will not be liable for punishment.

    -Under the Act, Court shall take cognisance of any offence under this Act only on the complaint made by
    - a Board or any other officer authorised in this behalf by it,   or
    - any person who has given notice of not less than sixty days, in the manner prescribed, of the alleged offence and of his intention to make a complaint, to the Board of officer authorised as aforesaid, And no Court inferior to that of a Metropolitan Magistrate or a Judicial Magistrate of the first Class shall try any offence punishable under this Act. Notwithstanding anything contained in Section 29 of the Code of Criminal Procedure, 1973, it shall be lawful for any Metropolitan Magistrate or a Judicial Magistrate of the first Class to pass a sentence of imprisonment for term exceeding two years or of fine exceeding two thousand rupees on any person convicted of an offence punishable under this Act.

23. Under the Act, members, officers and servants of Board shall be deemed to be public servants within the meaning

of Section 21 of the Indian Penal Code while acting or purporting to act in pursuance, of any of the provisions of this Act (45 of 1860) and the rules made there under.

24. The Act bars Civil Courts from exercising their jurisdiction to entertain any suit or proceeding in respect of any matter which an appellate authority constituted under this Act is empowered by under this Act to determine, and no injunction can be granted by any Court or other authority in respect of any action taken or to be taken in pursuance of any power conferred by or under this Act.

POWERS AND FUNCTIONS OF BOARDS
16. FUNCTIONS OF CENTRAL BOARD

(1) Subject to the provisions of this Act, the main function of the Central Board shall be to promote cleanliness of streams and wells in different areas of the States.

(2) In particular and without prejudice to the generality of the foregoing function, the Central Board may perform all or any of the following functions, namely:--

(a) Advise the Central Government on any matter concerning the prevention and control of water pollution;

(b) Co-ordinate the activities of the State Boards and resolve dispute among them;

(c) Provide technical assistance and guidance to the State Boards carry out and sponsor investigations and research relating to problems of water pollution and prevention, control or abatement of water pollution;

(d) Plan and organise the training of persons engaged or to be engaged in programs for the prevention, control or abatement of water pollution on such terms and conditions as the Central Board may specify;

(e) Organise through mass media a comprehensive programme regarding the prevention and control of water pollution;

[1][(ee) perform such of the functions of any State Board as may be specified in an order made under sub-section (2) of section 18];

(f) collect, compile and publish technical and statistical data relating to water pollution and the measures devised for its effective prevention and control and prepare manuals, codes or guides relating to treatment and disposal of sewage and trade effluents and disseminate information connected therewith;

(g) lay down, modify or annul, in consultation with the State Government concerned, the standards for a stream or well: Provided that different standards may be laid down for the same stream or well or for different streams or wells, having regard to the quality of water, flow characteristics of the stream or well and the nature of the use of the water in such stream or well or streams or wells;

(h) Plan and cause to be executed a nation-wide programme for the prevention, control or abatement of water pollution;

(i) Perform such other functions as may be prescribed.

(3) The Board may establish or recognise a laboratory or laboratories to enable the Board to perform its functions under this section efficiently, including the analysis of samples of water from any stream or well or of samples of any sewage or trade effluents.

17. FUNCTIONS OF STATE BOARD

(1) Subject to the provisions of this Act, the functions of a State Board shall be --

(a) to plan a comprehensive programme for the prevention, control or abatement of pollution of streams and wells in the State and to secure the execution thereof;

(b) to advise the State Government on any matter concerning the prevention, control or abatement of water pollution;

(c) to collect and disseminate information relating to water pollution and the prevention, control or abatement thereof;

(d) to encourage, conduct and participate in investigations and research relating to problems of water pollution and prevention, control or abatement of water pollution;

(e) to collaborate with the Central Board in organising the training of persons engaged or to be engaged in programmes relating to prevention, control or abatement of water pollution and to organise mass education programmes relating thereto;

(f) to inspect sewage or trade effluents, works and plants for the treatment or sewage and trade effluents and to review plans, specifications or other data relating to plants set up for the treatment of water, works for the purification thereof and the system for the disposal of sewage or trade effluents or in connection with the grant of any consent as required by this Act;

1. Ins. by Act 53 of 1988, s. S.

(g) lay down, modify or annul effluent standards for the sewage and trade effluents and for the quality of receiving waters (not being water in an inter-State stream) resulting from the discharge of effluents and to classify waters of the State;

(h) to evolve economical and reliable methods of treatment of sewage and trade effluents, having regard to the peculiar conditions of soils, climate and water resources of different regions and more specially the prevailing flow characteristics of water in streams and wells which render it impossible to attain even the minimum degree of dilution;

(i) to evolve methods of utilisation of sewage and suitable trade effluents in agriculture;

(j) to evolve efficient methods of disposal of sewage and trade effluents on land, as are necessary on account of the predominant conditions of scant stream flows that do not provide for major part of the year the minimum degree of dilution;

(k) to lay down standards of treatment of sewage and trade effluents to be discharged into any particular stream taking into account the minimum fair weather dilution available in that stream and the tolerance limits of pollution permissible in the water of the stream, after the discharge of such effluents;

(l) to make, vary or revoke any order-

(i) for the prevention, control or abatement of discharge of waste into streams or wells;

(ii) requiring any person concerned to construct new systems for the disposal of sewage and trade effluents or to modify, alter or extend any such existing system or to adopt such remedial measures as are necessary to prevent control or abate water pollution;

(m) to lay down effluent standards to be complied with by persons while causing discharge of sewage or both and to lay down, modify or annul effluent standards for the sewage and trade effluents;

(n) to advice the State Government with respect to the location of any industry the carrying on of which is likely to pollute a stream or well;

(o) to perform such other functions as may be prescribed or as may, from time to time be entrusted to it by the Central Board or the State Government.

(2) The Board may establish or recognise a laboratory or laboratories to enable the Board to perform its functions under this section efficiently, including the analysis of samples of water from any stream or well or of samples of any sewage or trade effluents.

18. POWERS TO GIVE DIRECTIONS

[2][(1)] In the performance of its functions under this Act-

(a) the Central Board shall be bound by such directions in writing the Central Government may give to it; and

(b) every State Board shall be bound by such directions in writing as the Central Government or the State Government may give to it:

Provided that where a direction given by the State Government is inconsistent with the direction given by the Central Board, the matter shall be referred to the Central Government for its decision.

[3][(2)] Where the Central Government is of the opinion that and State Board has defaulted in complying with any directions given by the Central Government under sub-section (1) and as a result of such default a grave emergency has arisen and it is necessary or expedient so to do in the public interest, it may, by order, direct the Central Board to perform any of the functions of the State Board in relation to such area for such period and for such purposes, as may be specified in the order.

(3) Where the Central Board performs any of the functions of the State Board in pursuance of a direction under sub-section (2), the expenses, if any, incurred by the Central Board with respect to performance of such functions may, if the State Board is empowered to recover such expenses, be recovered by the Central Board with interest (at such reasonable rate as the Central Government may, by order, fix) from the date when a demand for such expenses is made until it is paid from the person or persons concerned as arrears of land revenue or of public demand.

(4) For the removal of doubts, it is hereby declared that any directions to perform the functions of any State Board given under sub-section (2) in respect of any area would not preclude the State Board from performing such functions in any other area in the State or any of its other functions in that area.

2. S. 18 renumbered as sub-section (1) thereof by Act 53 of 1988, s. 9.
3. Ins. by s. 9, ibid.

PREVENTION AND CONTROL OF WATER POLLUTION
19. POWER OF STATE GOVERNMENT TO RESTRICT THE APPLICATION OF THE ACT TO CERTAIN AREAS

(1) Notwithstanding contained in this Act, if the State Government, after consultation with, or on the recommendation of, the State Board, is of opinion that the provisions of this Act need not apply to the entire State, it may, by notification in the Official Gazette, restrict the application of this Act to such area or areas as may be declared therein as water pollution, prevention and control area or areas and thereupon the provisions of this Act shall apply only to such area or areas.

(2) Each water pollution, prevention and control area may be declared either by reference to a map or by reference to the line of any watershed or the boundary of any district or partly by one method and partly by another.

(3) The State Government may, by notification in the Official Gazette-

(a) alter any water pollution prevention and control area whether by way of extension or reduction; or

(b) define a new water pollution, prevention and control area in which may be merged one or more water pollution, prevention and control areas, or any part or parts thereof.

20. POWER TO OBTAIN INFORMATION

(1) For the purpose of enabling a State Board to perform the function conferred on it by or under this Act, the State Board or any officer empowered by it in that behalf, may make surveys of any area and gauge and keep records of the flow or volume and other characteristics of an stream or well in such area, and may take steps for the measurement and recording of the rainfall in such area or any part thereof and for the installation and maintenance for those purposes of gauges or other apparatus and works connected therewith, and carry out stream surveys and may take such other steps as may be necessary in order to obtain any information required for the purposes aforesaid.

(2) A State Board may give directions requiring any person who in its opinion is abstracting water from any such stream or well in the area in quantities which are substantial in relation to the flow or volume of that stream or well or is discharging sewage or trade effluent into any such stream or well, to give such information as

to the abstraction or the discharge at such times and in such form as may be specified in the directions.

(3) Without prejudice to the provisions of sub-section (2), a State Board may, with a view to preventing or controlling pollution of water, give directions requiring any person in charge of any establishment where any [1][industry, operation or process, or treatment and disposal system is carried on, to furnish to it information regarding the construction, installation or operation of such establishment or of any disposal system or of any extension or addition thereto in such establishment and such other particulars as may be prescribed.

21. POWER TO TAKE SAMPLES OF EFFLUENTS AND PROCEDURE TO BE FOLLOWED IN CONNECTION THEREWITH

(1) A State Board or any officer empowered by it in this behalf shall have power to take for the purpose of analysis samples of water from any stream or well or samples of any sewage of trade effluent which is passing from any plant or vessel or from or over any place into any such stream or well.

(2) The result of any analysis of a sample of any sewage or trade effluent taken under sub-section (1) shall not be admissible in evidence in a legal proceeding unless the provisions of sub-sections (3), (4) and (5) are complied with.

(3) Subject to the provisions of sub-sections (4) and (5), when a sample (composite or otherwise as may be warranted by the process used) of any sewage or trade effluent is taken for analysis under sub-section (1), the person taking the sample shall --

(a) serve on the person in charge of, or having control over, the plant or vessel or in occupation of the place (which person is hereinafter referred to as the occupier) or any agent of such occupier, a notice, then and there in such form as may be prescribed of his intention to have it so analysed;

(b) in the presence of the occupier or his agent, divided the sample into two parts;

(c) cause each part to be placed in a container which shall be marked and sealed and shall also be signed both by the person taking the sample and the occupier or his agent;

(d) send one container forthwith-

(i) in a case where such sample is taken from any area situated in a Union territory, to the laboratory established or recognised by the Central Board under section; and

(ii) in any other case, to the laboratory established or recognised by the State Board under section 17;

(e) on the request of the occupier or his agent, send the second container --

(i) in a case where such sample is taken from any area situated in a Union territory, to the laboratory established or specified under sub-section (1) of section 51; and

(ii) in another case, to the laboratory established or specified under sub-section (1) of section 52.

[2][(4) When a sample of any sewage of trade effluent is taken for analysis under sub-section (1) and the person taking the sample serves on the occupier or his agent, a notice under clause (a) of sub-section (3) and the occupier or his agent wilfully absents himself, then --

(a) the sample so taken shall be placed in a container which shall be marked and sealed and shall also be signed by the person taking the sample and the same shall be sent forthwith by such person for analysis to the laboratory referred to in sub-clause (i) or sub- clause (ii), as the case may be, of clause (e) of sub-section (3) and such person shall inform the Government analyst appointed under sub-section (1) or sub-section (2), as the case may be, of section 53, in writing about the wilful absence of the occupier or his agent; and

(b) the cost incurred in getting such sample analysed shall be payable by the occupier or his agent and in case of default of such payment, the same shall be recoverable from the occupier or his agent, as the case may be, as an arrear of land revenue or of public demand:

Provided that no such recovery shall be made unless the occupier or, as the case may be, his agent has been given a reasonable opportunity of being heard in the matter.

(5) When a sample of any sewage or trade effluent is taken for analysis under sub-section (1) and the person taking the sample serves on the occupier or his agent a notice under clause (a) of sub-section (3) and the occupier or his agent who is present at the time of taking the sample does not make a request for dividing the

1. Subs. by Act 53 of 1988 s. 10 for "industry of trade"
2. Subs. by Act 44 of 1978, s. 10, for sub-section (4).

sample into two parts as provided in clause (b) of sub-section (3), then, the sample so taken shall be placed in a container which shall be marked and sealed and shall also be signed by the person taking the sample and the same shall be sent forthwith by such person for analysis to the laboratory referred to in sub-clause (i) or sub-clause (ii), as the case may be, of clause (d) of sub-section (3).

22. REPORTS OF RESULTS OF ANALYSIS ON SAMPLES TAKEN UNDER SECTION 21

(1) Where a sample of any sewage or trade effluent has been sent for analysis to the laboratory established or recognised by the Central Board or, as the case may be, the State Board, the concerned Board analyst appointed under sub-section (3) of section 53 shall analyse the sample and submit a report in the prescribed form of the result of such analysis in triplicate to the Central Board or the State Board, as the case may be.

(2) On receipt of the report under sub-section (1), one copy of the report shall be sent by the Central Board or the State Board, as the case may be, to the occupier or his agent referred to in section 21, another copy shall be preserved for production before the court in case any legal proceedings are taken against him and the other copy shall be kept by the concerned Board.

(3) Where a sample has been sent for analysis under clause (e) of sub-section (3) or sub-section (4) of section 21 to any laboratory mentioned therein, the Government analyst referred to in that sub-section shall analyse the sample and submit a report in the prescribed form of the result of the analysis in triplicate to the Central Board or, as the case may be, the State Board which shall comply with the provisions of sub-section (2).

(4) If there is any inconsistency or discrepancy between, or variation in the results of, the analysis carried out by the laboratory established or recognised by the Central Board or the State Board, as the case may be, and that of the laboratory established or specified under section 51 or section 52, as the case may be, the report of the latter shall prevail.

(5) Any cost incurred in getting any sample analysed at the request of the occupier or his agent shall be payable by such occupier or his agent and in case of default the same shall be recoverable from him as arrears of land revenue or of public demand.

23. POWER OF ENTRY AND INSPECTION

(1) Subject to the provisions of this section, any person empowered by a State Board in this behalf shall have a right at any time to enter, with such assistance as he considers necessary, any place-

(a) for the purpose of performing any of the functions of the Board entrusted to him;

(b) for the purpose of determining whether and if so in what manner, any such functions are to be performed or whether any provisions of this Act or the rules made there under of an notice, order, direction or authorisation served, made, given, or granted under this Act is being or has been complied with;

(c) for the purpose of examining any plant, record, register, document or any other material object or for conducting a search of any place in which he has reason to believe that an offence under this Act or the rules made there under has been or is being or is about to be committed and for seizing any such plant, record, register, document or other material object, if he has reason to believe that it may furnish evidence of the commission of an offence punishable under this Act or the rules made there under:

Provided that the right to enter under this sub-section for the inspection of a well shall be exercised only at reasonable hours in a case where such well is situated in any premises used for residential purposes and the water thereof is used exclusively for domestic purposes.

(2) The provisions of [3][the Code of Criminal Procedure, 1973, or, in relation to the State of Jammu and Kashmir, the provisions of any corresponding law in force in that State, shall, so far as may be, apply to an search or seizure under this section as they apply to any search or seizure made under the authority of a warrant issued under [4][section 94] of the said Code, or, as the case may be, under the corresponding provisions of the said law.

Explanation - For the purposes of this section, "place" includes vessel.

24. PROHIBITION ON USE OF STREAM OR WELL FOR DISPOSAL OF POLLUTING MATTER, ETC.

(1) Subject to the provisions of this section --

(a) no person shall knowingly cause or permit any poisonous, noxious or polluting matter determined in accordance with such standards as may be laid down by the State Board to enter (whether directly or indirectly) into any [5][stream or well or sewer or on land]; or

(b) no person shall knowingly cause or permit to enter into any stream any other matter which may tend, either directly or in combination with similar matters, to impede the proper flow of the water of the stream in a manner leading or likely to lead to a substantial aggravation of pollution due to other causes or of its consequences.

(2) A person shall not be guilty of an offence under sub-section (1), by reason only of having done any of the following acts, namely-

(a) constructing, improving a maintaining in or across or on the bank or bed of any stream any building, bridge, weir, dam, sluice, dock, pier, drain or sewer or other permanent works which he has a right to construct, improve or maintain;

(b) putting into an stream any sand or gravel or other natural deposit which has flowed from or been deposited by the current of such stream;

(c) causing or permitting, with the consent of the State Board, the deposit accumulated in a well, pond or reservoir to enter into any stream.

(3) The State Government may, after consultation with, or on the recommendation of, the State Board, exempt, by notification in the Official Gazette, any person from the operation of sub-section (1) subject to such conditions, if any, as may be specified in the notification and any conditions so specified may by a like notification and be altered, varied or amended.

25. RESTRICTIONS ON NEW OUTLETS AND NEW DISCHARGES

[6][(1) Subject to the provisions of this section, no person shall, without the previous consent of the State Board,--

(a) establish or take any steps to establish any industry, operation or process, or any treatment and disposal system or an extension or addition thereto, which is likely to discharge sewage or trade

3. Subs. by Act 44 of 1978, s. 11, for "Code of Criminal Procedure, 1898 (5 of 1898)"
4. Subs. by s. 11, ibid, for "section 98".
5. Subs. by Act 53 of 1988, s.11, for "stream or well".
6. Subs. by s. 12, Act 53 of 1988, for sub-sections (1) and (2).

effluent into a stream or well or sewer or on land (such discharge being hereafter in this section referred to as discharge of sewage); or

(b) bring into use any new or altered outlets for the discharge of sewage; or

(c) begin to make any new discharge of sewage;

Provided that a person in the process of taking any steps to establish any industry, operation or process immediately before the commencement of the Water (Prevention and Control of Pollution) Amendment Act, 1988, for which no consent was necessary prior to such commencement or, if he has made an application for such consent, within the said period of three months, till the disposal of such application.

(2) An application for consent of the State Board under sub-section (1) shall be made in such form, contain such particulars and shall be accompanied by such fees as may be prescribed.

(3) The State Board may make such inquiry as it may deem fit in respect of the application for consent referred to in sub-section (1) and in making any such inquiry shall follow such procedure as may be prescribed.

[7][(4) The State Board may -

(a) grant its consent referred to in sub-section (1), subject to such conditions as it may impose, being-

(i) in cases referred to in clauses (a) and (b) of sub-section (1) of section 25, conditions as to the point of discharge of sewage or as to the use of that outlet or any other outlet for discharge of sewage;

(ii) in the case of a new discharge, conditions as to the nature and composition, temperature, volume or rate of discharge of the effluent from the land or premises from which the discharge or new discharge is to be made; and

(iii) that the consent will be valid only for such period as may be specified in the order and any such conditions imposed shall be binding on any person establishing or taking any steps to establish any industry, operation or process, or treatment and disposal system or extension or addition thereto, or using the new or altered outlet, or discharging the effluent from the land or premises aforesaid; or

(b) refuse such consent for reasons to be recorded in writing.

7. Subs. by s. 12, Act 53 of 1988, for sub-sections (4), (5) and (6).

(5) Where, without the consent of the State Board, any industry operation or process, or any treatment and disposal system or any extension or addition thereto, is established, or any steps for such establishment have been taken or a new or altered outlet is brought into use for the discharge of sewage or a new discharge of sewage is made, the State Board may serve on the person who has established or taken steps to establish any industry, operation or process, or any treatment and disposal system or any extension or addition thereto, or using the outlet, or making the discharge, as the case may be, a notice imposing any such conditions as it might have imposed on an application for its consent in respect of such establishment, such outlet or discharge.

(6) Every State Board shall maintain a register containing particulars or conditions imposed under this section and so much of the register as relates to any outlet, or to any effluent, from any land or premises shall be open to inspection at all reasonable hours by any person interested in, or affected by such outlet, land or premises, as the case may be, or by any person authorised by him in this behalf and the conditions so contained in such register shall be conclusive proof that the consent was granted subject such conditions]

(7) The consent referred to in sub-section (1) shall, unless given or refused earlier, be deemed to have been given unconditionally on the expiry of a period of four months of the making of an application in this behalf complete in all respects to the State Board.

(8) For the purposes of this section and sections 27 and 30-

(a) the expression "new or altered outlet" means any outlet which is wholly or partly constructed on or after the commencement of this Act or which (whether so constructed or not) is substantially altered after such commencement;

(b) the expression "new discharge" means a discharge which is not, as respects the nature and composition, temperature, volume, and rate of discharge of the effluent substantially a continuation of a discharge made within the preceding twelve months (whether by the same or different outlet), so however that a discharge which is in other respects a continuation of previous discharge made as aforesaid shall not be deemed to be a new discharge by reason of any reduction of the temperature or volume or rate of discharge of the effluent as compared with the previous discharge.

26. PROVISION REGARDING EXISTING DISCHARGE OF SEWAGE OR TRADE EFFLUENT

Where immediately before the commencement of this Act any person was discharging any sewage or trade effluent into a [8][stream or well or sewer or on land], the provisions of section 25 shall, so far as may be, apply in relation to such person as they apply in relation to the person referred to in that section subject to the modification that the application for consent to be made under sub-section (2) of that section [9][shall be made on or before such date as may be specified by the State Government by notification in this behalf in the Official Gazette.

27. REFUSAL OR WITHDRAWAL OF CONSENT BY STATE BOARD

[10][(1) A State Board shall not grant its consent under sub-section (4) of section 25 for the establishment of any industry, operation or process, or treatment and disposal system or extension or addition thereto, or to the bringing into use of a new or altered outlet unless the industry, operation or process, or treatment and disposal system or extension or addition thereto, or the outlet is so established as to comply with an conditions imposed by the Board to enable it to exercise its right to take samples of the effluent.

[11][(2) A State Board may from time to time review-

[12][(a) any condition imposed under section 25 or section 26 and may serve on the person to whom a consent under section 25 or section 26 is granted a notice making any reasonable variation of or revoking any such condition.

(b) the refusal of any consent referred to in sub-section (1) of section 25 or section 26 or the grant of such consent without any condition, and may make such orders as it deemed fit]

(3) Any conditions imposed under section 25 or section 26 shall be subject to any variation made under sub-section (2) and shall continue in force until revoked under that sub-section.

28. APPEALS

(1) Any person aggrieved by an order made by the State Board under Section 25, section 26 or section 27 may within thirty days from the date on which the order is communicated to him, prefer an appeal to such authority (hereinafter referred to as the appellate authority) as the State Government may think fit to constitute:

Provided that the appellate authority may entertain the appeal after the expiry of the said period of thirty days if such authority is satisfied that the appellant was prevented by sufficient cause from filing the appeal in time.

[13][(2) An appellate authority shall consist of a single person or three persons as the State Government may think fit, to be appointed by that Government.

(3) The form and manner in which an appeal may be preferred under sub-section (1), the fees payable for such appeal and the procedure to be followed by the appellate authority shall be such as may be prescribed.

(4) On receipt of an appeal preferred under sub-section (1), the appellate authority shall, after giving the appellant and the State Board an opportunity of being heard, dispose of the appeal as expeditiously as possible.

(5) If the appellate authority determines that any condition imposed, or the variation of any

condition, as the case may be, was unreasonable, then-

(a) where the appeal is in respect of the unreasonableness of any condition imposed, such authority may direct either that the condition shall be treated as annulled or that there shall be substituted for it such condition as appears to it to be reasonable;

(b) where the appeal is in respect of the unreasonableness of any variation of a condition, such authority may direct either that the condition shall be treated as continuing in force unvaried or that it shall be varied in such manner as appears to it to be reasonable.

29. REVISION

(1) The State Government may at any time either of its own motion or on an application made to it in this behalf, call for the records of any case where an order has been made by the State Board under section 25, section 26 or section 27 for the purpose of satisfying itself as to the legality or propriety of any such order and may pass such order in relation thereto as it may think fit:

8. Subs. by Act 44 of 1978, s. 13, for "stream or well"
9. Subs. by s. 13, ibid., for certain words.
10. Subs. by Act 53 of 1988, s 13, for sub-section (1).
11. Subs. by Act 44 of 1978, s.] 4 for sub-section (2).
12. Subs. by Act 51 of 1988, s. 13, for cl. (a).
13. Subs. by Act 44 of 1978, s. for sub-section (2).

Provided that the State Government shall not pass any order under this sub-section without affording the State Board and the person who may be affected by such order a reasonable opportunity of being heard in the matter.

(2) The State Government shall not revise any order made under section 25, section 26 or section 27 where an appeal against that order lies to the appellate authority, but has not been preferred or where an appeal has been preferred such appeal is pending before the appellate authority.

30. POWER OF STATE BOARD TO CARRY OUT CERTAIN WORKS

[14][(1) Where under this Act, any conditions have been imposed on any person while granting consent under section 25 or section 26 and such conditions require such person to execute any work in connection therewith and such work has not been executed within such time as may be specified in this behalf, the State Board may serve on the person concerned a notice requiring him within such time (not being less than thirty days) as may be specified in the notice to execute the work specified therein]

(2) If the person concerned fails to execute the work as required in the notice referred to in

sub-section (1), then, after the expiration of the time specified in the said notice, the State Board may itself execute or cause to be executed such work.

(3) All expenses incurred by the State Board for the execution of the aforesaid work, together with interest, at such rate as the State Government may, by order, fix, from the date when a demand for the expenses is made until it is paid, may be recovered by that Board from the person concerned, as arrears of land revenue, or of public demand.

31. FURNISHING OF INFORMATION TO STATE BOARD AND OTHER AGENCIES IN CERTAIN CASES

[15][(1) If at any place where any industry, operation or process, or any treatment and disposal

system or any extension or addition thereto is being carried on, due to accident or other unforeseen act or event, any poisonous, noxious or polluting matter is being discharged, or is likely to be

14. Subs. by Act 53 of 1988, s. 14, for sub-section (1).
15. Subs. by s. 15, ibid., for sub-section (1).

discharged into a stream or well or sewer or on land and, as a result of such discharge, the water in any stream or well is being polluted, or is likely to be polluted, then the person incharge of such place shall forthwith intimate the occurrence of such accident, act or event to the State Board and such other authorities or agencies as may be prescribed]

(2) Where any local authority operates any sewerage system or sewage works the provisions of sub-section (1) shall apply to such local authority as they apply in relation to the person in charge of the place where an industry or trade is being carried on.

32. EMERGENCY MEASURES IN CASE OF POLLUTION OF STREAM OR WELL

(1) Where it appears to the State Board that any poisonous, noxious or polluting matter is present in [16][any stream or well or on land by reason of the discharge of such matter in such stream or well or on such land or has entered into that stream or well due to any accident or other unforeseen act or event, and if the Board is of opinion that it is necessary or expedient to take immediate action, it may for reasons to be recorded in writing, carry out such operations as it may consider necessary for all or any of the following purposes, that is to say-

(a) removing that matter from the [17][stream or well or on land and disposing it of in such manner as the Board considers appropriate;

(b) remedying or mitigating any pollution caused by its presence in the stream or well;

(c) issuing orders immediately restraining or prohibiting the persons concerned from discharging any poisonous, noxious or polluting matter [18][into the steam or well or on land or from making insanitary use of the stream or well.

(2) The power conferred by sub-section (I) does not include the power to construct any works other than works of a temporary character which are removed on or before the completion of the operations.

16. Subs. by Act 53 of 1988, s. 16, for "any stream or well".
17. Subs. by s, 16, ibid., for "stream or well".
18. Subs. by s. 16. ibid., for "into the stream or well".

33. POWER OF BOARD TO MAKE APPLICATION TO COURTS FOR RESTRAINING APPREHENDED POLLUTION OF WATER IN STREAMS OF WELLS

[19][(1) Where it is apprehended by a Board that the water in any stream or well is likely to be polluted by reason of the disposal or likely disposal of any matter in such stream or well or in any sewer, or on any land, or otherwise, the Board may make an application to a court, not inferior to that of a Metropolitan Magistrate or a Judicial Magistrate of the first class, for restraining the person who is likely to cause such pollution from so causing.]

(2) On receipt of an application under sub-section (I) the court make such order as it deems fit.

(3) Where under sub-section (2) the court makes an order restraining any person from polluting the water in any stream or well, it may in that order-

(i) direct the person who is likely to cause or has caused the pollution of the water in the stream or well, to desist from taking such action as is likely to cause pollution or, as the case may be, to remove such stream or well, such matter, and

(ii) authorise the Board, if the direction under clause (i) (being a direction for the removal of any matter from such stream or well) is not complied with by the person to whom such direction is issued, to undertake the removal and disposal of the matter in such manner as may be specified by the court.

(4) All expenses incurred by the Board in removing any matter in pursuance of the authorisation under clause (ii) of sub-section (3) or in the disposal of any such matter may be defrayed out of any money obtained by the Board from such disposal and any balance outstanding shall be recoverable from the person concerned as arrears of land revenue or of public demand.

[20][33A. POWER TO GIVE DIRECTIONS

Notwithstanding anything contained in any other law, but subject to the provisions of this Act, and to any directions that the Central Government may give in this behalf, a Board may, in the exercise of its powers and performance of its functions under this Act, issue any directions in writing to any person, officer or authority, and such person, officer or authority shall be bound to comply with such directions.

19. Subs. by s. 17, ibid., for sub-section (1).
20. Ins. by Act 53 of i988, s. IS.

Explanation- For the avoidance of doubts, it is hereby declared that the power to issue directions under this section includes the power to direct-

(a) the closure, prohibition or regulation of any industry, operation or process; or

(b) the stoppage or regulation of supply of electricity, water or any other service.]

5. THE AIR ACT (PREVENTION AND CONTROL OF POLLUTION), 1981
No. 14 of 1981 [29th March, 1981]

An Act to provide for the prevention, control and abatement of air pollution, for the establishment, with a view to carrying out the aforesaid purposes, of Boards, for conferring on and assigning to such Boards powers and functions relating thereto and for matters connected therewith. Whereas decisions were taken at the United Nations Conference on the Human Environment held in Stockholm in June, 1972, in which India participated, to take appropriate steps for the preservation of the natural resources of the earth which, among other things, include the preservation of the quality of air and control of air pollution; and whereas it is considered necessary to implement the decisions aforesaid in so far as they relate to the preservation of the quality of air and control of air pollution; be it enacted by Parliament in the Thirty-second Year of the Republic of India as follows-

CHAPTER I
PRELIMINARY

1. Short title, extent and commencement.

(1) This Act may be called the Air (Prevention and Control of Pollution) Act, 1981.

(2) It extends to the whole of India.

(3) It shall come into force on such date[1] as the Central Government may, by notification in the Official Gazette, appoint.

2. DEFINITIONS

In this Act, unless the context otherwise requires,-

(a) "air pollutant" means any solid, liquid or gaseous substance [[2](including noise)] present in the atmosphere in such concentration as may be or tend to be injurious to human beings or other living creatures or plants or property or environment;

(b) "air pollution" means the presence in the atmosphere of any air

(c) "approved appliances" means any equipment or gadget used for the bringing of any combustible material or for generating or consuming any fume, gas of particulate matter and approved by the State Board for the purpose of this Act;

(d) "approved fuel" means any fuel approved by the State Board for the purposes of this Act;

(e) "automobile" means any vehicle powered either by internal combustion engine or by any method of generating power to drive such vehicle by burning fuel;

(f) "Board" means the Central Board or State Board;

(g) "Central Board- means the [3][Central Board for the Prevention and Control of Water Pollution] constituted under section 3 of the Water (Prevention and Control of Pollution) Act, 1974;

(h) "chimney" includes any structure with an opening or outlet from or through which any air pollutant may be emitted,

(i) "control equipment" means any apparatus, device, equipment or system to control the quality and manner of emission of any air pollutant and includes any device used for securing the efficient operation of any industrial plant;

(j) "emission" means any solid or liquid or gaseous substance coming out of any chimney, duct or flue or any other outlet;

(k) "industrial plant" means any plant used for any industrial or trade purposes and emitting any air pollutant into the atmosphere;

(l) "member" means a member of the Central Board or a State Board, as the case may be, and

includes the Chairman thereof,

[4][(m) "occupier", in relation to any factory or premises, means the person who has control over the affairs of the factory or the premises, and includes, in relation to any substance, the person in possession of the substance;]

(n) "prescribed" means prescribed by rules made under this Act by the Central Government or as the case may be, the State government;

(o) "State Board" means-

(i) in relation to a State in which the Water (Prevention and Control of Pollution) Act,

1974, is in force and the State Government has constituted for that State a [5][State Board

for the Prevention and Control of Water Pollution] under section 4 of that Act, the said

State Board; and

(ii) in relation to any other State, the State Board for the Prevention and Control of Air

Pollution constituted by the State Government under section 5 of this Act.

1.16-5-1981: vide notification No. G.S.R. 351 (E), dated 15-5-1981,Gazette of India, Extraordinary, Part II, Section 3(i) page 944.
2. Ins. by Act 47 of 1987 (w..e.f. 1-4-1988).
3. The words in brackets "Central Board for the Prevention and Control of Water Pollution" shall be subs. as "Central Pollution Control Board" by Act 47 of 1987, s. 2 (w.e.f. 1.4.1988).

CHAPTER II
CENTRAL AND STATE BOARDS FOR THE PREVENTION AND CONTROL OF AIR POLLUTION
[6][3. Central Board for the Prevention and Control of Air Pollution

The Central Board for the Prevention and Control of Water Pollution constituted under section 3 of the Water (Prevention and Control of Pollution) Act, 1974 (6 of 1974), shall, without prejudice to the exercise and performance of its powers and functions under this Act, exercise the powers and perform the functions of the Central Board for the Prevention and Control of Air Pollution under this Act.]

[7][4. State Boards for the Prevention and Control of Water Pollution to be, State Boards for the Prevention and Control of Air Pollution

In any State in which the Water (Prevention and Control of Pollution) Act, 1974 (6 of 1974), is in force and the State Government has constituted for that State a State Board for the Prevention and Control of Water Pollution under section 4 of that Act, such State Board shall be deemed to be the State Board for the Prevention and Control of air Pollution constituted under section 5 of this Act and accordingly that State Board for the Prevention and Control of Water Pollution shall, without prejudice to the exercise and performance of its powers and functions under that Act, exercise the powers and perform the functions of the State Board for the Prevention and Control of Air Pollution under this Act.]

5. Constitution of State Boards

(1) In any State in which the Water (Prevention and Control of Pollution) Act, 1974 (6 of 1974), is not in force, or that Act is in force but the State Government has not constituted a [8][State Board for the Prevention and Control of Water Pollution] under that Act, the State Government shall, with effect from such date as it may, by notification in the Official Gazette, appoint, constitute a State

4. Subs. by Act 47 of 1987, s. 2, for cl. (m) (w.e.f. 1-4-1988).

5. The words in brackets "State Board for the Prevention and Control of Water pollution" shall be subs. as "State Pollution Control Board" s. 2 ibid. (date to be notified).

6. For sections 3 and 4, the following sections shall stand subs. by s.3 ibid., (date to be notified) namely :- 3. Central Pollution Control Board-The Central Pollution Control Board constituted under section 3 of the Water (Prevention and Control of Pollution) Act, 1974 (6 of 1974), shall, without prejudice to the exercise and performance of its powers and functions under that Act, exercise the powers and perform the functions of the Central Pollution Control Board for the prevention and control of air pollution under this Act.

Board for the Prevention and Control of Air Pollution under such name as may be specified in the notification, to exercise the powers conferred on, and perform the functions assigned to, that Board under this Act.

(2) A State Board constituted under this Act shall consist of the following members, namely:-

(a) A Chairman, being a person, having a person having special knowledge or practical experience in respect of matters relating to environmental protection, to be

nominated by the State Government: Provided that the Chairman may be either whole-time or part-time as the State Government may think fit;

(b) Such number of officials, not exceeding five, as the State Government may think fit, to be nominated by the State Government to represent that government;

(c) Such number of persons, not exceeding five, as the State Government may think fit, to be nominated by the State Government from amongst the members of the local authorities functioning within the State;

(d) Such number of non-officials, not exceeding three, as the State Government may think fit, to be nominated by the State Government to represent the interest of agriculture, fishery or industry or trade or labour or any other interest, which in the opinion of that government, ought to be represented;

(e) Two persons to represent the companies or corporations owned, controlled or managed by the State Government, to be nominated by that Government;

[9][(f) a full-time member-secretary having such qualifications knowledge and experience of scientific, engineering or management aspects of pollution control as may be prescribed, to be appointed by the State Governments Provided that the State Government shall ensure that not less than two of the members are persons having special knowledge or practical experience in, respect of matters relating to the improvement of the quality of air or the prevention, control or abatement of air pollution.]

7. State Pollution Control Boards constituted under section 4 of Act 6 of 1974 to be State Boards under this Act.-In any State in which the Water (Prevention and Control of Pollution) Ai-t, 1974, is in force and the State Government has constituted for that State a State Pollution Control Board under section 4 of that Act, such State Board shall be deemed to be the State Board for the Prevention and Control of Air Pollution constituted under section 5 of this Act, and accordingly that State Pollution Control Board shall Without prejudice to the exercise and performance of its powers and functions under that Act, exercise the powers and perform the functions of the State Board for the prevention and control of air pollution under this Act.

8. The words in brackets "State Board for the Prevention and Control of Water Pollution" shall be substituted as "State Pollution Control Board" by Act 47 of 1987, s. 4, (date to be notified).

9. Subs. by s. 4, ibid., for cl. (f) (w.e.f. 1-4-1988).

(3) Every State Board constituted under this Act shall be a body corporate with the name specified by the State Government in the notification issued under sub-section (1), having perpetual succession and a common seal with power, subject to the provisions of this Act, to acquire and dispose of property and to contract, and may by the said name sue or be sued.

6. Central Board to exercise the powers and perform die functions of a State Board in the Union territories

No State Board shall be constituted for a Union territory and in relation to a Union territory, the Central Board shall exercise the powers and perform the functions of a State Board under this Act for that Union territory Provided that in relation to any Union territory the Central Board may delegate all or any of its powers and functions under this section to such person or body of persons as the Central Government may specify.

7. Terms and conditions of service of members

(1) Save as otherwise provided by or under this Act, a member of a State Board constituted under this Act, other than the member-secretary, shall hold office for a term of three years from the date on which his nomination is notified in the Official Gazette: Provided that a member shall, notwithstanding the expiration of his term, continue to hold office until his successor enters upon his office.

(2) The terms of office of a member of a State Board constituted under this Act and nominated under clause (b) or clause (e) of sub-section (2) of section 5 shall come to an end as soon as he ceases to hold the office under the State Government as the case may be, the company or corporation owned, controlled or managed by the State Government, by virtue of which he was nominated.

(3) A member of a State Board constituted under this Act, other than the member- secretary, may at any time resign his office by writing under his hand addressed,-

(a) in the case of the Chairman, to the State Government; and

(b) in any other case, to the Chairman of the State Board, and the seat of be Chairman or such other member shall thereupon become vacant.

(4) A member of a State Board constituted under this Act, other than the member-secretary, shall be deemed to have vacated his

scat, if he is absent without reason, sufficient in the opinion of the State Board, from three consecutive meetings of the State Board or where he is nominated under clause (c) of subsection (2) of section 5, he ceases to be a member of the local authority and such vacation of scat shall, in either case, take effect from such as the State Government may, by notification in the Official Gazette, specify.

(5) A casual vacancy in a State Board constituted under this Act shall be filled by a fresh nomination and the person nominated to fill the vacancy shall hold office only for the remainder of die term for which the member whose place lie takes was nominated.

(6) A member of a State Board constituted under this Act shall be eligible for re-nomination [10]*****

(7) The other terms and conditions of service of the Chairman and other members (except the member-secretary) of a State Board constituted under this Act shall be such as may be prescribed.

8. Disqualifications

(1) No person shall be a member of a State Board constituted under this

(a) is, or at any time has been, adjudged insolvent, or

(b) is of unsound mind and has been so declared by a competent court,

(c) is, or has been, convicted of an offence which, in the opinion of the State Government, involves moral turpitude, or

(d) is, or at any time has been, convicted of an offence under this Act,

(e) has directly or indirectly by himself on by any partner.. any share or interest in any Finn or company carrying on the business of manufacture, sale, or hire of machinery, industrial plant, c6ntrol equipment or any other apparatus for the improvement of the quality of air or for the prevention, control or abatement of air pollution, or

(f) is a director or a secretary, manager or other salaried officer or employee of any company or firm having any contract with the Board, or with the Government constituting the Board or with a local authority in the State, or with a company or corporation owned, controlled or managed by the Government, for the carrying out of programmes for the improvement of the quality of air or for the prevention, control or abatement of air pollution, or

(g) has so abused, in the opinion Of the State Government, his position as a member,

as to render his continuance on the State Board detrimental to the interest of the general public.

(2) The State Government shall, by order in writing, remove any member who is, or has become, subject to any disqualification mentioned in sub-section M.

Provided that no order of removal shall be made by the State Government under this section unless the member concerned has been given a reasonable opportunity of showing cause against the same.

(3) Notwithstanding anything contained in sub-section (1) or sub-section (6) of section 7, a member who has been removed under this section shall not be eligible to continue to hold office until his successor enters upon his office, or, as the case may be, for re-nomination as a member.

9. Vacation of seats by members

If a member of a State Board constituted under this Act becomes subject to any of the disqualifications specified in section 8, his seat shall become vacant.

10. Meetings of Board

(1) For the purposes of this Act, a Board shall meet at least once in every three months and shall observe such rules of procedure in regard to the transaction of business at its meetings as may be prescribed: Provided that it, in the opinion of the Chairman, any business of an urgent nature is to be transacted, he may convene a meeting of the Board at such time as he thinks fit for the aforesaid purpose.

(2) Copies of minutes of the meetings under sub-section (1) shall be forwarded to the Central Board and to the State Government concerned.

11. Constitution of committees

(1) A Board may constitute as many committees consisting wholly of members or partly of members and partly of other persons and for such purpose or purposes as it may think fit.

(2) A committee constituted under this section shall meet at such time and at such place, and shall observe such rules of procedure

10. The words "but not for more than two terms" omitted by Act 47 of 1987, s. 5 (w.e.f. 1.4.1988)

in regard to the transaction of business at its meetings, as may be prescribed.

(3) The members of a committee other than the members of the Board shall be paid such fees and allowances, for attending its meetings and for attending to any other work of the Board as may be prescribed.

12. Temporary association of persons with Board for particular purposes

(1) A Board may associate with itself in such manner, and for such purposes, as may be prescribed, any person whose assistance or advice it may desire to obtain in performing any of its functions under this Act.

(2) A person associated with the Board under sub-section (1) for any purpose shall have a right to take part in the discussions of the Board relevant to that purpose, but shall riot have a tight to vote at a meetings of the Board and shall not be a member of the Board for any other

purpose.

(3) A person associated with a Board under sub-section (1) shall be entitled to receive such fees and allowances as may be prescribed.

13. Vacancy in Board not to invalidate acts or proceedings

No act or proceeding of a Board or any committee thereof shall be called in question on the ground merely of the existence of any vacancy in or any defect in the constitution of, the Board or such committee, as the case may be.

14. Member-secretary and officers and other employees of State Boards

(1) The terms and conditions of service of the member-secretary of a State Board constituted under this Act shall be such as may be prescribed.

[11][(2) The member-secretary of a State Board, whether constituted under this Act or not, shall exercise such powers and perform such duties as may be prescribed or as may, from time to time, be delegated to him by the State Board or its Chairman.]

(3) subject to such rules as may be made by the State Government in this behalf, a State Board, whether constituted under this Act or not, may appoint such officers and other employees as it considers

necessary for the efficient performance of its functions under this Act.

(4) The method of appointment, the conditions of service and the scale of pay of the officers (other than the member-secretary) and other employees of a State Board appointed under sub-section (3) shall be such as may be determined by regulations made by the State Board under
this Act.

(5) Subject to such conditions as may be prescribed, a State Board constituted under this Act may from time to time appoint any qualified person
to be a consultant to the Board and pay him such salary and allowances or fees, as it thinks fit.

15. Delegation of powers
A State Board may, by general or special order, delegate to t1he Chairman or the member-secretary or any other officer of the Board subject to such conditions and limitations, if any. as may be specified in the order, such of its powers and functions under this Act as It may deem necessary.

CHAPTER III
POWERS AND FUNCTIONS OF BOARDS
16. Functions of Central Board
(1) Subject to the provisions of this Act, and without prejudice to the performance, of its functions under the Water (Prevention and Control of Pollution) Act, IL974 (6 of 1974), the main functions of the Central Board shall be to improve the quality of air and to prevent, control or abate air pollution in the country.

(2) In particular and without prejudice to the generality of the foregoing functions, the Central Board may-

(a) Advise the Central Government on any matter concerning the improvement of the quality of air and the prevention, control or abatement of air pollution;

(b) Plan and cause to be executed a nation-wide programme for the prevention, control or abatement of air pollution;

(c) Co-ordinate the activities of the State and resolve dispute among them;

(d) Provide technical assistance and guidance to the State Boards, carry out and sponsor investigations and research relating to problems of air pollution and prevention, control or abatement of air pollution;

[12][(dd) perform such of the function of any State Board as may be specified in and order made under sub-section (2) of section 18;]

(e) Plan and organise the training of persons engaged or to be engaged in programmes for the prevention, control or abatement of air pollution on such terms and conditions as the Central Board may specify;

(f) Organise through mass media a comprehensive programme regarding the prevention, control or abatement of air pollution;

(g) Collect, compile and publish technical and statistical data relating to air pollution and the measures devised for its effective prevention, control or abatement and prepare manuals, codes or guides relating to prevention, control or abatement of air pollution;

(h) Lay down standards for the quality of air.,

(i) Collect and disseminate information in respect of matters relating to air pollution;

(j) Perform such other functions as may be prescribed.

(3) The Central Board may establish or recognise a laboratory or laboratories to enable the Central Board to perform its functions under this section efficiently.

(4) The Central Board may-

(a) Delegate any of its functions under this Act generally or specially to any of the committees appointed by it;

(b) Do such other things and perform such other acts as it may think necessary for the proper discharge of its functions and generally for the purpose of carrying into effect the purposes of this Act.

17. Functions of State Boards

(1) Subject to the provisions of this Act, and without prejudice to the performance of its functions, if any, under the Water (Prevention and Control of Pollution) Act, 1974 (Act 6 of 1974), the functions of a State Board shall be-

(a) To plan a comprehensive programme for the prevention, control or abatement of air pollution and to secure the execution thereof-

(b) To advise the State Government on any matter concerning the prevention, control or abatement of air pollution;

11. Subs. by Act 47 of 1987, -. 6, for sub-section (2) (w.e.f. 1-4-1988).
12. Ins. by Act 47 of 1987. s. 7 (w.e.f. 1-4-1988).

(c) To collect and disseminate information relating to air pollution;

(d) To collaborate with the Central Board in organising the training of persons
engaged or to be engaged in programmes relating to prevention, control or abatement of air pollution and to organise mass-education programme relating thereto;

(e) To inspect, at all reasonable times, any control equipment, industrial plant or manufacturing process and to give, by order, such directions to such persons as it may consider necessary to take steps for the prevention, control or abatement of air pollution;

(f) To inspect air pollution control areas at such intervals as it may think necessary, assess the quality of air therein and take steps for the prevention, control or abatement of air pollution in such areas;

(g) to lay down, in consultation with the Central Board and having regard to the standards for the quality of air laid down by the Central Board, standards for emission of air pollutants into the atmosphere from industrial plants and automobiles or for the discharge of any air pollutant into the atmosphere from any other source whatsoever not being a ship or an aircraft: Provided that different standards for emission may be laid down under this clause for different industrial plants having regard to the quantity and composition of emission of air pollutants into the atmosphere from such industrial plants;

(h) to advise the State Government with respect to the suitability of any premises or location for carrying on any industry which is likely to cause air pollution;

(i) to Perform such other functions as may be prescribed or as may, from time to time, be entrusted to it by the Central Board or the State Government;

(j) to do such other things and to perform such other acts as it may think necessary for the proper discharge of its functions and generally for the purpose of carrying into effect the purposes of this Act.

(2) A State Board may establish or recognise a laboratory or laboratories to enable the State Board to perform its functions under this section efficiently.

18. Power to give directions

[13][(1) In the performance of its functions under this Act-

(a) the Central Board shall be bound by such directions in writing as the Central Government may give to it; and

(b) every State Board shall be bound by such directions in writing as the Central Board or the State Government may give to it: Provided that where a direction given by the State Government is inconsistent with the direction given by the Central Board, the matter shall be referred to the Central Government for its decision.]

[14][(2) Where the Central Government is of the opinion that any State Board has defaulted in complying with any directions given by the Central Board under sub-section (1) and as a result of such default a grave emergency has arisen and it is necessary or expedient so to do in the public interest, it m4y, by order, direct the Central Board to perform any of the functions of the State Board in relation to such area, for such period and for such purposes, as may be specified in the order.

(3) Where the Central Board performs any of the functions of the State Board in pursuance of a direction under sub-section (2), the expenses, if any incurred by the Central Board with respect to the performance of such functions may, if the State Board is empowered to recover such expenses, be recovered by the Central Board with interest (at such reasonable rate as the Central Government may, by order, fix) from the date when a demand for such expenses is made until it is paid from the person or persons concerned as arrears of land revenue or of public demand.

(4) For the removal of doubts, it is hereby declared that any directions to perform the functions of any State Board given under sub-section (2) in respect of any area would not preclude the State Board from performing such functions in any other area in the State or any of its other functions in that area.]

---

13. S. 18 renumbered as sub-section (1) thereof by Act 47 of 1987, s. 8 (w.e.f. 1-4-1988).
14. Ins. by s. 8, ibid. (w.e.f. 1-4-1988).

CHAPTER IV
PREVENTION AND CONTROL OF AIR POLLUTION
19. Power to declare air pollution control areas,
(1) The State Government may, after consultation with the State Board, by notification in the Official Gazette declare in such manner as may be prescribed, any area or areas within the State as air pollution control area or areas for the purposes of this Act.
(2) The State government may, after consultation with the State Board, by notification in the Official Gazette-
(a) Alter any air pollution control area whether by way of extension or reduction;
(b) Declare a new air pollution control area in which may be merged one or more existing air pollution control areas or any part or parts thereof.
(3) If the State Government, after consultation with the State Board, is of opinion that the use of any fuel, other than an approved fuel, in any air pollution control area or part thereof, may cause or is likely to cause air pollution, it may, by notification in the Official Gazette, prohibit the use of such fuel in such area or part thereof with effect from such date (being not less than three months from the date of publication of the notification) as may be specified in the notification.
(4) The State Government may, after consultation with the State Board, by notification in the Official Gazette, direct that with effect fr6m such date as may be specified therein, no appliance, other than an approved appliance, shall be used in the premises situated in an air pollution control area: Provided that different dates may be specified for different parts of an air pollution control area or for the use of different appliances.
(5) If the State Government, after consultation with the State Board, is of opinion that the burning of any material (not being fuel) in any air pollution control area or part thereof may cause or is likely to cause air pollution, it may, by notification in the Official Gazette, prohibit the burning of such material in such area or part thereof.

20. Power to give instructions for ensuring standards for emission from automobiles
With a view to ensuring that the standards for emission of air pollutants from automobiles laid down by the State Board tinder clause (g) of subsection (1) of section 17 are complied with,

the State Government shall, in consultation with the State Board, give such instructions as may be deemed necessary to the concerned authority in charge of registration of motor vehicles under the Motor Vehicles Act, 1939 (Act 4 of 1939), and such authority shall, notwithstanding anything contained in that Act or the rules made there under be bound to comply with such instructions.

21. Restrictions on use of certain industrial plants

[15][(1) Subject to the provisions of this section, no person shall, without the previous consent of the State Board, establish or operate any industrial plant in an air pollution control area: Provided that a person operating any industrial plant in any air pollution control area,

immediately before the commencement of section 9 of the Air (Prevention and Control of Pollution) Amendment Act, 1987, for which no consent was necessary prior to such commencement, may continue to do so for a period of three months from such commencement or, if he has made an application for such consent within the said period of three months, till the disposal of such application.]

(2) An application for consent of the State Board under sub-section (1) shall be accompanied by such fees as may be prescribed 'and shall be made in the prescribed form and shall contain the particulars of the industrial plant and such other particulars as may be prescribed: Provided that where any person, immediately before the declaration of any area as an air pollution control area, operates in such area any industrial plant, [16]*** such person shall make the application under this sub-section within such period (being not less than three months from the date of such declaration) as may be prescribed and where such person makes such application, he shall be deemed to be operating such industrial plant with the consent of the State Board until the consent applied for has been refused,

(3) The State Board may make such inquiry as it may deem fit in respect of the application for consent referred to in sub-section (1) and in making any such inquiry, shall follow such procedure as may be prescribed.

(4) Within a period of four months after the receipt of the application for consent referred to in sub-section (1), the State

15. Subs. by Act 47 of 1987, s. 9, for sub-section (1) (w.e.f. 1-4-1988).

Board shall, by order in writing, [17][and for reasons to be recorded in the order, grant the consent applied for subject to such conditions and for such period as may be specified in the order, or refuse consent:]

[18][Provided that it shall be open to the State Board to cancel such consent before the expiry of the period for which it is granted or refuse further consent after such expiry if the conditions subject to which such consent has been granted are not fulfilled:

Provided further that before cancelling a consent or refusing a further consent under the first provision, a reasonable opportunity of being heard shall be given to the person concerned.]

(5) Every person to whom consent has been granted by the State Board under sub-section (4), shall comply with the following conditions, namely-

(i) The control equipment of such specifications as the State Board may approve in this behalf shall be installed and operated in the premises where the industry is carried on or proposed to be carried on;

(ii) The existing control equipment, if any, shall be altered or replaced in accordance with the directions of the State Board;

(iii) The control equipment referred to in clause (i) or clause (ii) shall be kept at all times in good running condition;

(iv) Chimney, wherever necessary, of such specifications as the State Board may approve in this behalf shall be erected or re-erected in such premises; .and

(v) Such other conditions as the State Board, may specify in this behalf,

(vi) The conditions referred to in clauses (i), (ii) and (iv) shall be complied with within such period as the State Board may specify in this behalf-

Provided that in the case of a person operating any industrial plant [19]*** in an air pollution control area immediately before the date of declaration of such area as an air pollution control area, the period so specified shall not be less than six months :

Provided further that-

(a) After the installation of any control equipment in accordance with the specifications under clause (i), or

(b) After the alteration or replacement of any control equipment in

16. Certain words omitted by s. 9, ibid., (w.e.f. 1-4-1988).
17. Subs. by Act 47 of 1987, s. 9, for certain words (w.e.f. 1-4-1988).
18. Ins. by s. 9, ibid. (w.e.f. 1-4-1988).

accordance with the directions of the State Board under clause (ii), or

(c) After the erection or re-erection of any chimney under clause (iv), no control equipment or chimney shall be altered or replaced or, as the case may be, erected or re-created except with the previous approval of the State Board.

(6) If due to any technological improvement or otherwise the State Board is of opinion that all or any of the conditions referred to in sub-section

(5) Require or requires variation (including the change of any control equipment, either in whole or in part), the State Board shall, after giving the person to whom consent has been granted an opportunity of being heard, vary all or any of such conditions and thereupon such person shall be bound to comply with the conditions as so varied.

(7) Where a person to whom consent has been granted by the State Board under sub-section (4) transfers his interest in the industry to any other person, such consent shall be deemed to have been granted to such other person and he shall be bound to comply with all the conditions subject to which it was granted as if the consent was granted to him originally.

22. Persons carrying on industry, etc., and to allow emission of air pollutants in excess of the standard laid down by State Board

No person [20]**** operating any industrial plant, in any air pollution control area shall discharge or cause or permit to be discharged the emission of any air pollutant in excess of the standards laid down by the State Board under clause (g) of sub-section (1) of section 17.

[21][22A. Power of Board to make application to court for restraining person from causing air pollution

(1) Where it is apprehended by a Board that emission of any air pollutant, in excess of the standards laid down by the State Board under clause (g) of sub-section (1) of section 17, is likely to occur by reason of any person operating an industrial plant or otherwise in any air pollution control area, the Board may make an application to a court, not inferior to that of a Metropolitan Magistrate or a Judicial Magistrate of the first class for restraining such person from emitting such air pollutant.

(2) On receipt of the application under sub-section (1), the court may make such order as it deems fit.

(3) Where under sub-section (2), the court makes an order restraining any person from to be discharged the emission of any air pollutant, it may, in that order,-

(a) direct such person to desist from taking such action as is likely to cause emission;

(b) authorise the Board, if the direction under clause (a) is no , t complied with by the person to whom such direction is issued, to implement the direction in such manner as may be specified by the court.

(4) All expenses incurred by the Board in implementing the & sections of the court under clause (b) of sub-section (3) sl) all be recoverable from the person concerned as an-ears of land revenue or of public demand.

23. Furnishing, of information to State Board and other agencies in certain cases

(1) Where in any [22]*** area the emission of any air pollutant into the atmosphere in excess of the standards laid down by the State Board occurs or is apprehended to occur due to accident or other unforeseen act or event, the person in charge of the premises from where which emission occurs or is apprehended to occur shall forthwith intimate the fact of such occurrence or the apprehension of such occurrence to the State Board and to such authorities or agencies as may be prescribed.

(2) On receipt of information with respect to the fact or the apprehension of any occurrence of the nature referred to in sub-section (1), whether through intimation under that sub-section or otherwise, the State Board and the authorities or agencies shall, as early as practicable, cause such remedial measure to be taken as are necessary to mitigate the emission of such air pollutants.

(3) Expenses, if any, incurred by the State Board, authority or agency with respect to the remedial measures referred to in sub-section (2) together with interest ("t such reasonable rate, as the State Government may, by order, fix) from the date when a demand for the expenses is made until it is paid, may be recovered by that Board, authority or agency from the person concerned, as arrears of land revenue, or of public demand.

19. Certain words omitted by Act 47 of 1987,s. 9, (w.e.f. 1-4-1988).
20. Certain words omitted by Act 47 of 1987, s. 10 . (w.e.f. 1-4-1998)
21. Ins by s. 11, ibid. (w.e.f. 1-4-1988).

24. Power of entry and inspection

(1) Subject to the provisions of this section, any person empowered by a State Board in this behalf shall have a right to enter, at all reasonable times with such assistance as he considers necessary, any place-

(a) for the purpose of performing any of the functions of the State Board entrusted to him:

(b) for the purpose of determining whether and if so in what manner, any such functions are to be performed or whether any provisions of this Act or the rules made there under or any notice, order, direction or authorisation served, made, given or granted under this Act is being or has been complied with;

(c) for the purpose of examining and testing any control equipment, industrial plant, record, register, document or any other material object or for conducting a search of any place in which he has reason to believe that an offence under this Act or the rules made has been or is being or is about to be committed and for seizing any such control equipment, industrial plant, record, register, document or other material object if he has reasons to believe that it may furnish evidence of the commission of an offence punishable under this Act or the rules made there under.

(2) Every person [23]*** operating any control equipment or any industrial plant, in an air pollution control area shall be bound to render all assistance to the person empowered by the State Board under sub-section (1) for carrying out the functions under that sub-section and if he fails to do so without any reasonable cause or excuse, he shall be guilty of an offence under this Act.

(3) If any person wilfully delays or obstructs any person empowered by the State Board under sub-section (1) in the discharge of his duties, he shall be guilty of an offence under this Act.

(4) The provisions of the Code of Criminal Procedure, 1973, or, in relation to the State of Jammu and Kashmir, or any area, in which that Code is not in force, the provisions of any corresponding law in force in that State or area, shall, so far as may be, apply to any search or seizure under this section as they apply to any search or seizure made under the authority of a warrant issued under section 94 of the said Code or, as the case may be, under the corresponding provisions of the said law.

22. The words "air pollution control" omitted by s. 12, ibid., (w.e.f. 1-4-1988).

23. Certain words omitted by Act 47 of 1987, s. 13 (w.e.f. 1-4-1988).

25. Power to obtain information

For the purposes of carrying out the functions entrusted to it, the State Board or any officer empowered by it in Ns behalf may call for any information (including information regarding the types of air pollutants emitted into the atmosphere and the level of the emission of such air pollutants) from the occupier or any other person carrying oil any industry or operating any control equipment or industrial plant and for the purpose of verifying the correctness of such information, the State Board or such officer shall have the right to inspect the premises where such industry, control equipment or industrial plant is being carried on or operated.

26. Power to take samples of air or emission and procedure to be followed in connection therewith.

(1) A State Board or any officer empowered by it in this behalf shall have power to take, for the purpose of analysis, samples of air or emission from any chimney, flue or duct or any other outlet in such manner as may be prescribed.

(2) The result of any analysis of a sample of emission taken under subsection (1) shall not be admissible in evidence in any legal proceeding unless the provisions of sub-sections (3) and (4) are complied with.

(3) Subject to the provisions of sub-section (4), when a sample of emission is taken for analysis under sub-section (1), the person taking the sample shall-

(a) serve on the occupier or his agent, a notice, then and there, in such form as may be prescribed, of his intention to have it so analysed;

 (b) in the presence of the occupier or his agent, collect a sample of emission for analysis;

(c) cause the sample to be placed in a container or containers which shall be marked and sealed and shall also be signed both by the person taking the sample and the occupier or his agent;

(d) send, without delay, the container to the laboratory established or recognised by the State Board under section 17 or, if a request in that behalf is made by the occupier or his agent when the notice is served on him under clause (a), to the laboratory established or specified under sub-section (1) of section 28.

(4) when a sample of emission is taken for analysis under sub-section (1) and the person taking the sample serves on the

occupier or his agent, a notice under clause (a) of sub-section (3), then-

(a) in a case where the occupier or his agent wilfully absents himself, the person taking the sample shall collect the sample of emission for analysis to be placed in a container or containers which shall be marked and sealed and shall also be signed by the person taking the sample, and

(b) in a case where the occupier or his agent is present at the time of taking the sample but refuses to sign the marked and scaled container or containers of the sample of emission as required under clause (c) of subsection (3), the marked and sealed container or containers shall be signed by the person taking the sample, and the container or containers shall be sent without delay by the person 'Caking the sample for analysis to the laboratory established or specified under sub-section (7) of section 28 and such person shall inform the Government analyst appointed under sub-section (1) of section 29, in writing, about the wilful absence of the occupier or his agent, or, as the case may be, his refusal to sing the container or containers.

27. Reports of the result of analysis on samples taken under section 26

(1) Where a sample of emission has been sent for analysis to the laboratory established or recognised by the State Board, the Board analyst appointed under sub-section (2) of section 29 shall analyse the sample and submit a report in the prescribed form of such analysis in triplicate to the State Board.

(2) On receipt of the report under sub-section (1), one copy of the report shall be sent by the State Board to the occupier or his agent referred to in section 26, another copy shall be preserved for production before the court in case any legal proceedings are taken against him and the other copy shall be kept by the State Board.

(3) Where a sample has been sent for analysis under clause (a~ of sub-section (3) or sub-section (4) of section 26 to any laboratory mentioned therein, the Government analyst referred to in the said sub-section (4) shall analyse the sample and submit a report in the prescribed form of the result of the analysis in triplicate to the State Board which shall comply with the provisions of sub-section (2).

(4) Any cost incurred in getting any sample analysed at the request of the occupier or his agent as provided in clause (d) of sub-section (3) of section 26 or when he wilfully absents himself or refuses to sing the marked and scaled container or containers of sample of emission under subsection (4) of that section, shall be payable by such occupier or his agent and in case of default the same shall be recoverable from him as arrears of land revenue or of public demand.

28. State Air Laboratory
(1) The State Government may, by notification in the Official Gazette-

(a) Establish one or more State Air Laboratories; or

(b) Specify one or more laboratories or institutes as State Air Laboratories to carry out the functions entrusted to the State Air Laboratory under this Act.

(2) The State Government may, after consultation with the State Board, make rules prescribing-

(a) the functions of the State Air Laboratory;

(b) the procedure for the submission to the said Laboratory of samples of air or emission for analysis or tests, the form of the Laboratory's report thereon and the fees payable in respect of such report;

(c) such other matters as may be necessary or expedient to enable that Laboratory to carry out its functions.

29. Analysis
(1) The State Government may, by notification in the Official Gazette, appoint such persons as it thinks fit and having the prescribed qualifications to be government analysts for the purpose of analysis of samples of air or emission sent for analysis to any laboratory established or specified under sub-section (1) of section 28.

(2) Without prejudice to the provisions of section 14, the State Board may, by notification in the Official Gazette, and with the approval of the State Government, appoint such persons as it thinks fit and having the prescribed qualifications to be Board analysts for the purpose of analysis of samples of air or emission sent for analysis to any laboratory established or recognised under section 17.

30. Reports of analysis

Any document purporting to be a report signed by a Government analyst or, as the case may be, a State Board analyst may be used as evidence of the facts stated therein in any proceeding under this Act.

31. Appeals

(1) Any person aggrieved by an order made by the State Board under this Act may, within thirty day from the date on which the order is communicated to him, prefer an appeal to such authority (hereinafter referred to as the Appellate Authority) as the State government may think fit to constitute : Provided that the Appellate Authority may entertain the appeal after tile expiry of the said period of thirty days if such authority is satisfied that the appellant was prevented by sufficient cause from filing the appeal in time.

(2) The Appellate Authority shall consist of a single person or three persons as the State Government may think fit to be appoint by the State Government.

(3) The form and the manner in which an appeal may be preferred under subsection (1), the fees payable for such appeal and the procedure to be followed by the Appellate Authority shall be such as may be prescribed.

(4) On receipt of an appeal preferred under sub-section (1), the Appellate Authority shall, after giving the appellant and the State Board an opportunity of being heard, dispose of the appeal as expeditiously as possible.

[24][31A. Power to give directions

Notwithstanding anything contained in any other law, but subject to the provisions of this Act, and to any directions that the Central Government may give in this behalf, a Board may, in the exercise of its powers and performance of its functions under this Act, issue any directions in writing to any person, officer or authority, and such person, officer or authority shall be bound to comply with such directions.

Explanation-For the avoidance of doubts, it is hereby declared that tile power to issue directions under this section, includes the power to direct-

(a) The closure, prohibition or regulation of any industry, operation or

(b) The stoppage or regulation of supply of electricity, water or any other service.]

CHAPTER V
FUND, ACCOUNTS AND AUDIT
32. Contribution by Central Government

The Central Government may, after due appropriation made by Parliament by law in this behalf make in each financial year such contributions to the State Boards as it may think necessary to enable the State Board to perform their functions under this Act: Provided that noting in this section shall apply to any [25][State Board for the Prevention and Control of water Pollution] constituted under section 4 of the Water (Prevention and Control of Pollution) Act, 1974, which is empowered by that Act to expend money from its fund there under also for performing its functions, under any law for the time being in force relating to the prevention, control or abatement of air pollution.

33. Fund of Board

(1) Every State Board shall have its own fund for the purposes of this Act and all sums which may, from time to time, be paid to it by the Central Government and all other receipts (by way of contributions, if any, from the State Government, fees, gifts, grants, donations benefactions or otherwise) of that Board shall be carried to the fund of the Board and all payments by the Board shall be made there from.

(2) Every State Board may expend such sums as it thinks fit for performing its functions under this Act and such sums shall be treated as expenditure payable out of the fund of that Board.

(3) Nothing in this section shall apply to any [25][State Board for the Prevention and Control of Water Pollution] constituted under section 4 of the Water (Prevention and Control of Pollution) Act, 1974, which is empowered by that Act to expend money from its fund there under also for performing its functions under any law for the time being in force relating to the prevention., control or abatement of air pollution.

[26] [33A. Borrowing powers of Board

A Board may, with the consent of, or in accordance with the terms of any general or special authority given to it by, the Central Government or, as the case may be, the State

24. Ins. by Act 47 of 1987, s. 14 (w.e.f. 1-4-1988).
25. The Words in brackets "State Board for the Prevention and control of Water Pollution" shall be substituted as "State Pollution Control Board"

Government, borrow money from any source by way of loans or issue of bonds, debentures or such other instruments, as it may deem fit, for discharging all or any of its functions under this Act.]

34. Budget

The Central Board or as the case may be the State Board shall, during each financial year, prepare, in such form and at such time as may be prescribed, a budget in respect of the financial year next ensuing showing the estimated receipt and expenditure under this Act, and copies thereof shall be forwarded to the Central Government or, as the case may be, the State Government.

[27] [35. Annual report

(1) The Central Board shall, during each financial year, prepare, in such form as may be prescribed, an annual report giving full account of its activities under this Act during the previous financial year and copies thereof shall be forwarded to the Central Government
within four months from the last date of the previous financial year and that Government shall cause every such report to be laid before both Houses of Parliament within nine months of the last date of the previous financial year.

(2) Every State Board shall, during each financial year, prepare, in such fort-n as may be prescribed, an annual report giving full account of its activities under this Act during the previous financial year and copies thereof shall be forwarded to the State Government within four months from the last date of the previous financial year and that Government shall cause every such report to be laid before the State Legislature within a period of nine months from the date of the previous financial year.)

36. Accounts and audit

(1) Every Board shall, in relation to its functions under this Act, maintain proper accounts and other relevant records and prepare an annual statement of accounts in such form as may be prescribed by the Central Government or, as the case may be, the State Government.

(2) The accounts of the Board shall be audited by an auditor duly qualified to act as an auditor of companies under section 226 of the Companies Act, 1956.

26. Ins. by Act 47 of 1987, s. 16 (w.e.f. 1-4-1988).
27. Subs. by Act 47 of 1987, s. 17, for s. 35 (w.e.f. 1-4-1988).

(3) The said auditor shall be appointed by the Central Government or, as the case may be, the State Government on the advice of the Comptroller and Auditor General of India.

(4) Every auditor appointed to audit the accounts of the Board under this Act shall have the right to demand the production of books, accounts, connected vouchers and other documents and papers and to inspect any of the offices of the Board.

(5) Every such auditor shall send a copy of his report together with an audited copy of the accounts to the Central Government or, as the case may be, the State Government.

(6) The Central Government shall, as soon as may be after the receipt of the audit report under sub-section (5), cause the same to be laid before both Houses of Parliament.

(7) The State Government shall, as soon as may be after the receipt of the audit report under sub-section (5), cause the same to be laid before the State Legislature.

CHAPTER VI
PENALTIES AND PROCEDURE
[28][37. Failure to comply with the provisions of section 21 or section 22 or with the directions issued under section 31A

(1) whoever fails to comply with the provisions of section 21 or section 22 or directions issued under section 3 1 A, shall, in respect of each such failure, be punishable with imprisonment for a terms which shall not be less than one year and six months but which may extend to six years and with fine, and in case the failure continues, with an additional fine which may extend to five thousand rupees for every day during which such failure continues after the conviction for the first such failure.

(2) if the failure referred to in sub-section (1) continues beyond a period of one year after the date of conviction, the offender shall be punishable with imprisonment for a term which shall not be less than two years but which may extend to seven years and with fine.]

38. Penalties for certain acts
Whoever-

(a) destroys, pulls down, removes, injures or defaces any pillar, post or stake fixed in the ground or any notice or other matter put up, inscribed or placed, by or under the authority of the Board, or

28. Subs. by Act. 47 of 1987, s. 18, for s. 37 (w.e.f. 1-4-1988).

(b) Obstructs any person acting under the orders or directions of the Board from exercising his powers and performing his functions under this Act, or

(c) Damages any works or property belonging to the Board, or

(d) Fails to furnish to the Board or any officer or other employee of the Board any information required by the Board or such officer or other employee for the purpose of this Act, or

(e) Fails to intimate the occurrence of the emission of air pollutants into the atmosphere in excess of the standards laid down by the State Board or the apprehension of such occurrence,

to the State Board and other prescribed authorities or agencies as required under sub-section

(1) of section 23, or

(f) in giving any information which he is required to give under this Act, makes a statement which is false in any material particular, or

(g) for the purpose of obtaining any consent under section 21, makes a statement which is false in any material particular shall be punishable with imprisonment for a term which may extend to three months or with fine which may extend to [29][ten thousand rupees] or with both.

[30][39. Penalty for contravention of provisions of the Act

Whoever contravenes any of the provisions of this Act or any order or direction issued there under, for which no penalty has been elsewhere provided in this Act, shall be punishable with imprisonment for a term which may extend to three months or with fine which may extend to ten thousand rupees or with both, and in the case of continuing contravention, with an additional fine which may extend to five thousand, rupees for every day during which such contravention continues after conviction for the first such contravention.)

40. Offences by companies

(1) Where an offence under this Act has, been committed by a company, every person who, at the time the offence was committed, was directly in charge of, and was responsible to, the company for the conduct of the business of the company, as well as the company, shall be deemed to be guilty of the offence and shall be liable to be proceeded against and punished accordingly:

29. Subs. by Act 47 of,1987, s. 19, for "five hundred rupees" (w.e.f. 1-4-1988).
30. Subs. bv s. 20. ibid., for s. 39 (w.e.f. 1-4-1988).

Provided that nothing contained in this sub-section shall render any such person liable to any punishment provided in this Act, if he proves that the offence was committed without his knowledge or that he exercised all due diligence to prevent the commission of such offence.

(2) Notwithstanding anything contained in sub-section (1), where an offence under this Act has been committed by a company and it is proved that the offence has been committed with the consent or connivance of, or is attributable to any neglect on the part of, any director, manager, secretary or other officer of the company, such director, manager, secretary or other officer shall also be deemed to be guilty of that offence and shall be liable to be proceeded against and punished accordingly.

Explanation -For the purpose of this section,-

(a) "Company" means anybody corporate, and includes a firm or other association of individuals; and

(b) "Director", in relation to a firm, means a partner in the firm.

41. Offences by Government Departments

(1) Where an offence under this Act has been committed by any Department of Government, the Head of the Department shall be deemed to be guilty of the offence and shall be liable to be proceeded against and punished accordingly: Provided that nothing contained in this section shall render such Head of the Department liable to any punishment if he proves that the offence was committed without his knowledge or that he exercised all due diligence to prevent the commission of such offence.

(2) Not withstanding anything contained in sub-section (1), where an offence under this Act has been committed by a Department of Government and it is proved that the offence has been committed with the consent or connivance of, or is attributable to any neglect on the part of, any officer, other than the Head of the Department, such officer shall also be deemed to be guilty of that offence and shall be liable to be proceeded against and punished accordingly. ,

42. Protection of action taken in good faith

No suit, prosecution or other legal proceeding shall lie against the Government or any officer of the Government or any member or any officer or other employee of the Board in respect of anything which is done or intended to be done in good faith in pursuance of Otis Act or the rules made there under.

[31][43. Cognizance of offences

(1) No court shall take cognizance of any offence under this Act except on a complaint made by-

(a) a Board or any officer authorised in this behalf by it; or

(b) any person who has given notice of not less than sixty days, in the manner prescribed, of the alleged offence and of his intention to make a complaint to the Board or officer authorised as aforesaid, and no court inferior to that of a Metropolitan Magistrate or a Judicial Magistrate of the first class shall try any offence punishable under this Act.

(2) Where a complaint has been made under clause (b) of sub-section (1), the Board shall, on demand by such person, make available the relevant reports in its possession

to that person: Provided that the Board may refuse to make any such report available to such person if the same is, in its opinion, against the public interest.]

44. Members, officers and employees of Board to be public servants

All the members and all officers and other employees of a Board when acting or purporting to act in pursuance of any of the provisions of this Act or the rules made there under shall be deemed to be public servant within the meaning of section 21 of the Indian Penal Code (45 of 1860).

45. Reports and returns

The Central Board shall, in relation to its functions under this Act, furnish to the Central Government, and a State Board shall, in relation to its functions under this Act, furnish to the State government and to the Central Board such reports, returns, statistics, accounts and other information as that Government, or, as the case may be, the Central Board may, from time to time, require.

46. Bar of jurisdiction

No civil court shall have jurisdiction to entertain any suit or proceeding in respect of any matter which an Appellate

31. Subs. by Act 47 of 1987, s. 21, for s. 43 (w.e.f. 1-4-1988).

Authority constituted under this Act is empowered by or under this Act to determine, and no injunction shall be granted by any court or other authority in respect of any action taken or to be taken in pursuance of any power conferred by or under this Act.

CHAPTER VII
MISCELLANEOUS

47. Power of Central Government to supersede State Board-
(1) If at any time the State Government is of opinion-

(a) That a State Board constituted under this Act has persistently made default in the performance of the functions imposed on it by or under this Act, or

(b) That circumstances exist which render it necessary in the public interest so to do, the State Government may, by notification in the Official Gazette, supersede the State Board for such period, not exceeding six months, as may be specified in the notification: Provided that before issuing a notification under this sub-section for the reasons mentioned in clause (a), the State Government shall give a reasonable opportunity to the State Board to show cause why it should not be superseded and shall consider the explanations and objections, if any, of the State Board.

(2) Upon the publication of a notification under sub-section (1) superseding the State Board,-

(a) All the members shall, as from the date of supersession, vacate their offices as such;

(b) All the powers, functions and duties which may, by or under this Act, be exercised, performed or discharged by the State Board shall, until the State Board is reconstituted under sub-section (3), be exercised, performed or discharged by such person or persons as the State Government may direct.

(c) All property owned or controlled by the State Board shall, until the Board is reconstituted under sub-section (3), vest in the State Government.

(3) On the expiration of the period of supersession specified in the notification issued under sub-section (1), the State Government may-

(a) Extend the period of supersession for such further term, not exceeding six months, as it may consider necessary; or

(b) Reconstitute the State Board by a fresh nomination or appointment as the case may be and in such case any person who vacated his office under clause (a) of sub-section (2) shall also be eligible for nomination or appointment. Provided that the State Government may at any time before the expiration of the period of supersession whether originally specified under subsection (1) or as extended under this sub-section, take action under clause (b) of this sub-section.

48. Special provision in the case of supersession of the Central Board or the State Boards constituted under the Water (Prevention and Control of Pollution) Act, 1974

Where the Central Board or any State Board constituted under the Water (Prevention and Control of Pollution) Act, 1974 (Act 6 of 1974), is superseded by the Central Government or the State Government, as the case may be, under that Act, all the powers, functions and duties of the Central Board or such State Board under this Act shall be exercised, performed or discharged during the period of such supersession by the person or persons, exercising, performing or discharging the powers, functions and duties of the Central Board or such State Board under the Water (Prevention and Control of Pollution) Act, 1974, during such period.

49. Dissolution of State Boards constituted under the Act

(1) As and when the Water (Prevention and Control of Pollution) Act, 1974 (Act 6 of 1974), comes into force in any State and the State Government constitutes a I [State Board for the Prevention and Control of Water Pollution] under that Act, the State Board constituted by the
State Government under this Act shall stand dissolved and the Board first-mentioned shall exercise the powers and perform the functions of the Board second-mentioned in that State,
(2) On the dissolution of the State Board constituted under this Act-
(a) All the members shall vacate their offices as such;
(b) All moneys and other property of whatever kind (including the fund of the State Board) owned by, or vested in, the State Board, immediately before such dissolution, shall stand transferred to and vest in the [32][State Board for the Prevention and Control of Water Pollution];
(c) Every officer and other employee serving under the State, Board immediately before such dissolution shall be transferred to

and become an officer or other employee of the [32][State Board for the Prevention and Control of Water Pollution] and hold office by the same
tenure and at the same remuneration and on the same terms and conditions of service as he would have held the same if the State Board constituted under this Act had not been dissolved
and shall continue to do so unless and until such tenure, remuneration and conditions of service are duly altered by the [State Board for the Prevention and Control of Water Pollution] :

Provided that the tenure, remuneration and terms and conditions of service of any such officer or other employee shall not be altered to his disadvantage without the previous sanction of the State Government;

(d) all liabilities obligations of the State Board of whatever kind, immediately before such dissolution, shall be deemed to be the liabilities or obligations, as the case may be, of the
[33][State Board for the Prevention and Control of Water Pollution] and any proceeding or cause of action, pending or existing immediately before such dissolution by or against the State Board constituted under this Act in relation to such liability or obligation may be continued and enforced by or against the 1[State Board for the Prevention and Control of Water Pollution.]

50. [Power to amend the Schedule.]

Rep. by the Air (Prevention and Control of Pollution) Amendment Act, 1987 (47 of 1987), s. 22 (w.e.f. 1-4-1988).

51. Maintenance of register

(1) Every State Board shall maintain a register containing particulars of the persons to whom consent has been granted under section 21, the standard for emission laid down by it in relation to each such consent and such other particulars as may be prescribed.

(2) The register maintained under sub-section (1) shall be open to inspection at all reasonable hours by any person interested in or affected by such standards for emission or by any other person authorised by such person in this behalf.

32. The Words in brackets "State Board for the Prevention and control of Water Pollution" shall be substituted as "State Pollution Control Board" by Act 47 of 1987, s. 15 (date to be notified).
33. The Words in brackets "State Board for the Prevention and Control of Water Pollution", shall be substituted as "State Pollution Control Board" by Act 47 of 1987, s. 15 (date to be notified).

52. Effect of other laws

Save as otherwise provided by or under the Atomic Energy Act, 1962 (33 of 1962), in relation to radioactive air pollution the provisions of this Act shall have effect notwithstanding anything inconsistent therewith contained in any enactment other than this Act.

53. Power of Central Government to make rules

(1) The Central Government may, in consultation with the Central Board by notification in the Official Gazette, make rules in respect of the following matters namely :-

(a) The intervals and the time and place at which meetings of the Central Board or any committee thereof shall be held and the procedure to be followed at such meetings, including the quorum necessary for the transaction of business thereat, under sub-section (1) of section 10 and under sub-section (2) of section 11;

(b) the fees and allowances to be paid to the members of a committee of the Central Board, not being members of the Board, under sub-section (3) of section 11;

(c) the manner in which and the purposes for which persons may be associated with the Central Board under sub-section (1) of section 12;

(d) the fees and allowance to be paid under sub-section (3) of section 12 to persons associated with the Central Board under subsection (/) of section 12;

(e) the functions to be performed by the Central Board under clause (j) of sub-section (2) of section 16;

[34][(f) the form in which and the time within which the budget of the Central Board may be prepared and forwarded to the Central Government under section 34;

(ff) the form in which the annual report of die Central Board may be prepared under section 35;1

(g) the form in which the accounts of the Central Board may be maintained under sub-section (1) of section 36.

(2) Every rule made by the Central Government under this Act shall be laid, as soon as may be after it is made, before each House of Parliament, while it is in session, for a total period of thirty days which may be comprised in one session or in two or more successive sessions, and if, before the expiry of the session immediately following the session or the successive sessions aforesaid, both Houses agree in making any modification in the

rule or both Houses agree that the rule should not be made, the rule shall thereafter have effect only in such modified form or be of no effect, as the case may be; so, however, that any such modification or annulment shall be without prejudice to the validity of anything previously done under that rule.

54. Power of State Government to make rules

(1) Subject to the provisions of sub-section (3), the State Government may, by notification in the Official Gazette, make rules to carry out the purposes of this Act in respect of matter not falling within the purview of section 53.

(2) In particular, and without prejudice to the generality of the foregoing power, such rules may provide for all or any of the following matters, namely --

[35][(a) the qualifications, knowledge and experience of scientific, engineering or management aspect of pollution control required for appointment as member-secretary of a State Board constituted under the Act;]

[36][(aa) the terms and conditions of service of the Chairman and other members (other than the member-secretary) of the State Board constituted under this Act under sub-section (7) of section 7;

(b) The intervals and the time and place at which meetings of the State Board or any committee thereof shall be held and the procedure to be followed at such meetings, including the quorum necessary for the transaction of business thereat, under sub-section (1) of

section 10 and under sub-section (2) of section 11;

(c) the fees and allowances to be paid to the members of a committee of the State Board, not being members of the Board under subsection (3) of section 11;

(d) the manner in which and the purpose for which persons may be associated with the State Board under sub-section (1) of section 12;

(e) The fees and allowances to be paid under sub-section (3) of section 12 to persons associated with the State Board under sub-section (1) of section 12;

34. Subs. by Act 47 of 1987, s. 23, for cl. (f) (w.e.f. 1-4-1988).
35. Ins by Act 47 of 1987, s. 24, (w.e.f. 1-4-1988).
36. Act (p) renumbered as cl. (aa) by s. 24, ibid. (w.e.f. 1-4-1988).

(f) The terms and conditions of service of the member-secretary of a State Board constituted under this Act under sub-section (1) of section 14;

(g) The powers and duties to be exercised and discharged by the member-secretary of a State Board under sub-section (2) of section 14;

(h) The conditions subject to which a State Board may appoint such officers and other employees as it considers necessary for the efficient performance of its functions under sub-section (3) of section 14;

(i) The conditions subject to which a State Board may appoint a consultant under sub-section (5) of section 14;

(j) The functions to be performed by the State Board under clause (i) of sub-section (1) of section 17;

(k) The manner in which any area or areas may be declared as air pollution control area or areas under sub-section (1) of section 19;

(l) The form of application for the consent of the State Board, the fees payable therefore, the period within which such application shall be made and the particulars it may contain, under sub-section (2) of section 21;

(m) The procedure to be followed in respect of an inquiry under subsection (3) of section 2 1;

(n) The authorities or agencies to whom information under sub-section (1) of section 23 shall be furnished;

(o) The manner in which samples of air or emission may be taken under sub-section (1) of section 26;

(p) The form of the notice referred to in sub-section (3) of section 26;

(q) The form of the report of the State Board analyst under sub-section (1) of section 27;

(r) The form of the report of the Government analyst under sub-section (3) of section 27;

(s) The functions of the State Air Laboratory, the procedure for the submission to the said Laboratory of samples of air or emission for analysis or tests, the form of Laboratory's report thereon, the fees payable in respect of such report and other matters as may be necessary or expedient to enable that Laboratory to carry out its functions, under sub-section (2) of section 28;

(t) The qualifications required for Government analysts under subsection (1) of section 29;

(u) The qualification required for State Board analysts under sub-section (2) of section 29;

(v) The form and the manner in which appeals may be preferred, the fees payable in respect to such appeals and the procedure to be followed by the Appellate Authority in disposing of the appeals under sub-section (3) of section 31;

[37][(w) the form in which and the time within which the budget of the State Board may be prepared and forwarded to the State Government under section 34;

(ww) the form in which the annual report of the State Board may be prepared under section 35,1(x) the form in which the accounts of the State Board may be maintained under the sub-section (1) of section 36;

[38][(xx) the manner in which notice of intention to make a complaint shall be given under section 43;]

(y) The particulars which the register maintained under section 51 may contain;

(z) Any other matter which has to be, or may be, prescribed.

(3) After the first constitution of the State Board, no rule with respect to any of the matters referred to in sub-section (2) other than those referred to 39[in clause (aa) thereof], shall be made, varied, amended or repealed without consulting that Board.

[The Schedule.] Omitted by the air (Prevention and Control of Pollution) Amendment Act, 1987, s. 25 (w.e.f. 1-4-1988).

---

37. Subs. by AcL 47 of 1987, s. 24. for cl. (w) (wx.f. 1-4-1988).
38. Ins. by Ac, 47 of 1987, s. 24 (w.e.f. 1-4-1988).
39. Subs. by s. 24, ibid., for "in clause (a)" (w.e.f 1-4-1988).

6. THE NOISE POLLUTION
(REGULATION AND CONTROL) RULES, 2000
MINISTRY OF ENVIRONMENT & FORESTS
NOTIFICATION
New Delhi, the 14th February, 2000

[1][S.O.123(E) – Whereas, the increasing ambient noise level in public places from various sources, inter-alia, industrial activity, construction activity, [2][fire crackers, sound producing instruments], generator sets, loud speakers, public address systems, music systems, vehicular horns and other mechanical devices have deleterious effects on human health and the psychological well being of the people; it is considered necessary to regulate and control of noise producing and generating sources with the objective of maintaining the ambient air quality standards in respect of noise;

Whereas, a draft of Noise Pollution (Regulation and Control) Rule, 1999 was published under the notification of the Government of India in the Ministry of Environment and Forests vide number S.O.528 (E), dated the 28th June, 1999 inviting objections and suggestions from all the persons likely to be affected thereby, before the expiry of the period of sixty days from the date on which the copies of the Gazette containing the said notification are made available to the public;

And, whereas, copies of the said Gazette were made available to the public on the 1st day of July, 1999;

And, whereas the objections and suggestions received from the public in respect of the said draft rules have been duly considered by the Central Government; Now, therefore, in exercise of the powers conferred by clause (ii) of sub-section (2) of section 3, sub-section (1) and clause (b) of sub-section (2) of section 6 and section 25 of the Environment (Protection) Act, 1986 (29 of 1986) read with Rule 5 of the Environment (Protection) Rules, 1986, the Central Government hereby makes the following rules for the regulation and control of noise producing and generating sources, namely-

The Noise Pollution (Regulation and Control) Rules, 2000
1. SHORT-TITLE AND COMMENCEMENT-
(1) These rules may be called the Noise Pollution (Regulation and Control) Rules, 2000.

(2) They shall come into force on the date of their publication in the Official Gazette.

2. DEFINITIONS-

In these rules, unless the context otherwise requires,-

(a) "Act" means the Environment (Protection) Act, 1986 (29 of 1986);

(b) "area/zone" means all areas which fall in either of the four categories given in the Schedule annexed to these rules;

[3][(c) "authority" means and includes any authority or officer authorized by the Central Government, or as the case may be, the State Government in accordance with the laws in force and includes a District Magistrate, Police Commissioner, or any other officer not below the rank of the Deputy Superintendent of Police designated for the maintenance of the ambient air quality standards in respect of noise under any law for the time being in force];

[4][(d) "court" means a governmental body consisting of one or more judges who sit to adjudicate disputes and administer justice and includes any court of law presided over by judge, judges or a magistrate and acting as a tribunal in civil, taxation and criminal cases;

(e) "educational institution" means a school, seminary, college, university, professional academies, training institutes or other educational establishment, not necessarily a chartered institution and includes not only buildings, but also all grounds necessary for the accomplishment of the full scope of educational instruction, including those things essential to mental, moral and physical development;

(f) "hospital" means an institution for the reception and care of sick, wounded, infirm or aged persons, and includes government or private hospitals, nursing homes and clinics;]

[5][(g) "person" shall include any company or association or body of individuals, whether incorporated or not;]

[6][(h) "State Government" in relation to a Union territory means the Administrator thereof appointed under article 239 of the Constitution;]

[7][(i) "public place" means any place to which the public have access, whether as of right or not, and includes auditorium, hotels, public waiting rooms, convention centres, public offices, shopping malls,

cinema halls, educational institutions, libraries, open grounds and the like which are visited by general public; and

(j) "night time" means the period between 10.00 p.m. and 6.00 a.m.]

3. AMBIENT AIR QUALITY STANDARDS IN RESPECT OF NOISE FOR DIFFERENT AREAS/ZONES-

(1) The ambient air quality standards in respect of Noise for different areas/zones shall be such as specified in the Schedule annexed to these rules.

(2) The State Government [8][shall categorize] the areas into industrial, commercial, residential or silence areas/zones for the purpose of implementation of noise standards for different areas.

(3) The State Government shall take measures for abatement of noise including noise emanating from vehicular movements, [9][blowing of horns, bursting of sound emitting fire crackers, use of loud speakers or public address system and sound producing instruments]

and ensure that the existing noise levels do not exceed the ambient air quality standards specified under these rules.

(4) All development authorities, local bodies and other concerned authorities while planning developmental activity or carrying out functions relating to town and country planning shall take into consideration all aspects of noise pollution as a parameter of quality of life to avoid noise menace and to achieve the objective of maintaining the ambient air quality standards in respect of noise.

(5) An area comprising not less than 100 meters around hospitals, educational institutions and courts may be declared as silence area/zone for the purpose of these rules.

1. As published in the Gazette of India, Extraordinary, Part II- Section 3(ii), vide S.O. 123(E), dated 14.2.2000.
2. Inserted by Rule 2 of the Noise Pollution (Regulation and Control) (Amendment) Rules, 2010 notified vide S.O.50 (E), dated 11.01.2010.
3. Substituted by Rule 2(i) of the Noise Pollution (Regulation and Control) Amendment Rules, 2000 notified vide S.O. 1046(E), dated 22.11.2000, w.e.f. 22.11.2000.
4. Inserted by Rule 2(iii), of the Noise Pollution (Regulation and Control) Amendment Rules, 2000 notified vide S.O.
1046(E), dated 22.11.2000, w.e.f. 22.11.2000.
5. Re-numbered and substituted by Rule 2(ii) of the Noise Pollution (Regulation and Control) (Amendment) Rules, 2000 notified vide S.O.1046(E), dated 22.11.2000, w.e.f. 22.11.2000.
6. Renumbered by Rule 2(ii), ibid.
7. Inserted by Rule 3 of the Noise Pollution (Regulation and Control) (Amendment) Rules, 2010 notified vide S.O. 50 (E), dated 11.01.2010.
8. Substituted by Rule 3 of the Noise Pollution (Regulation and Control) (Amendment) Rules, 2000 notified vide S.O.1046(E), dated 22.11.2000, w.e.f. 22.11.2000.

4. RESPONSIBILITY AS TO ENFORCEMENT OF NOISE POLLUTION CONTROL MEASURES-

(1) The noise levels in any area/zone shall not exceed the ambient air quality standards in respect of noise as specified in the Schedule.

(2) The authority shall be responsible for the enforcement of noise pollution control measures and the due compliance of the ambient air quality standards in respect of noise.

[10][(3) The respective State Pollution Control Boards or Pollution Control Committees in consultation with the Central Pollution Control Board shall collect, compile and publish technical and statistical data relating to noise pollution and measures devised for its effective prevention, control and abatement.]

5. RESTRICTIONS ON THE USE OF LOUD SPEAKERS/PUBLIC ADDRESS SYSTEM [11][AND SOUND PRODUCING INSTRUMENTS]-

(1) A loud speaker or a public address system shall not be used except after obtaining written permission from the authority.

[12][(2) A loud speaker or a public address system or any sound producing instrument or a musical instrument or a sound amplifier shall not be used at night time except in closed premises for communication within, like auditoria, conference rooms, community halls, banquet halls or during a public emergency.]

[13][(3) Not withstanding anything contained in sub-rule (2), the State Government may subject to such terms and conditions as are necessary to reduce noise pollution, permit use of loud speakers or [14][public address systems and the like during night hours] (between 10.00 p.m. to 12.00 midnight) on or during any cultural or religious festive occasion of a limited duration not exceeding fifteen days in all during a calendar year.]

[15][The Concerned State Government shall generally specify in advance, the number and particulars of the days on which such exemption would be operative].

10. Inserted by Rule 2 (i) of the Noise Pollution (Regulation and Control) Amendment Rules, 2006 notified vide S.O.1569(E), dated 19.9.2006.
11. Inserted by Rule 5(i) of the Noise Pollution (Regulation and Control) (Amendment) Rules, 2010 notified vide S.O.50(E), dated 11.01.2010.
12. Substituted by Rule 5(ii) of the Noise Pollution (Regulation and Control) (Amendment) Rules, 2010 notified vide S.O.50 (E), dated 11.01.2010.
13. Inserted by Rule 2 of the Noise Pollution (Regulation and Control) Amendment Rules, 2002 notified vide Notification S.O. 1088(E), dated 11.10.2002.
14. Substituted by Rule 5(iii)(a) of the Noise Pollution (Regulation and Control) (Amendment) Rules, 2010 notified vide S.O.50 (E), dated 11.01.2010.
15. Inserted by Rule 5(iii) (b) of the Noise Pollution (Regulation and Control) (Amendment) Rules, 2010 notified vide S.O.50 (E), dated 11.01.2010.

[16][(4) The noise level at the boundary of the public place, where loudspeaker or public address system or any other noise source is being used shall not exceed 10 dB (A) above the ambient noise standards for the area or 75 dB(A) whichever is lower.

(5) The peripheral noise level of a privately owned sound system or a sound producing instrument shall not, at the boundary of the private place, exceed by more than 5 dB(A) the ambient noise standards specified for the area in which it is used].

[17][5A. RESTRICTIONS ON THE USE OF HORNS, SOUND EMITTING CONSTRUCTION EQUIPMENTS AND BURSTING OF FIRE CRACKERS-

(1) No horn shall be used in silence zones or during night time in residential areas except during a public emergency.

(2) Sound emitting fire crackers shall not be burst in silence zone or during night time.

(3) Sound emitting construction equipments shall not be used or operated during night time in residential areas and silence zones.]

6. CONSEQUENCES OF ANY VIOLATION IN SILENCE ZONE/AREA-

Whoever, in any place covered under the silence zone/area commits any of the following offence, he shall be liable for penalty under the provisions of the Act:-

(i) Whoever, plays any music or uses any sound amplifiers,

(ii) Whoever, beats a drum or tom-tom or blows a horn either musical or pressure, or trumpet or beats or sounds any instrument,

(iii) whoever, exhibits any mimetic, musical or other performances of a nature to attract crowds,

[18][(iv) whoever, bursts sound emitting fire crackers; or

(v) whoever, uses a loud speaker or a public address system.]

---

16. Inserted by Rule 5(iv) of the Noise Pollution (Regulation and Control) (Amendment) Rules, 2010 notified vide S.O.50 (E), dated 11.01.2010.
17. Inserted by Rule 6 of the Noise Pollution (Regulation and Control) (Amendment) Rules, 2010 notified vide S.O.50 (E), dated 11.01.2010.
18. Inserted by Rule 7 of the Noise Pollution (Regulation and Control) (Amendment) Rules, 2010 notified vide S.O.50(E), dated 11.01.2010.

7. COMPLAINTS TO BE MADE TO THE AUTHORITY-

(1) A person may, if the noise level exceeds the ambient noise standards by 10 dB(A) or more given in the corresponding columns against any area/zone [19][or, if there is a violation of any provision of these rules regarding restrictions imposed during night time], make a complaint to the authority.

(2) The authority shall act on the complaint and take action against the violator in accordance with the provisions of these rules and any other law in force.

8. POWER TO PROHIBIT ETC. CONTINUANCE OF MUSIC SOUND OR NOISE-

(1) If the authority is satisfied from the report of an officer incharge of a police station or other information received by him [20][including from the complainant] that it is necessary to do so in order to prevent annoyance, disturbance, discomfort or injury or risk person who dwell or occupy property on the vicinity, he may, by a written order issue such directions as he may consider necessary to any person for preventing, prohibiting, controlling or regulating:-

(a) The carrying on in or upon, any premises of –

(i) Any vocal or instrumental music,

(ii) Sounds caused by playing, beating, clashing, blowing or use in any manner whatsoever of any instrument including loudspeakers, [21][public address systems, horn, construction equipment, appliance or apparatus] or contrivance which is capable of producing or re-producing sound,

[22][(iii) sound caused by bursting of sound emitting fire crackers, or]

(b) The carrying on in or upon, any premises of any trade, a vocation or operation or process resulting in or attended with noise.

(2) The authority empowered under sub-rule (1) may, either on its own motion, or on the application of any person aggrieved by an order made under sub-rule (1), either rescind, modify or alter any such order: Provided that before any such application is disposed of, the said authority shall afford to the applicant [23][and to the original complainant, as the case may be] an opportunity of appearing before it either in person or by a person representing him and showing cause against the order and shall, if it rejects any

such application either wholly or in part, record its reasons for such rejection.

Note: The principal rules were published in the Gazette of India vide number, S.O.123(E), dated 14th February, 2000 and subsequently amended vide S.O.1046(E), dated 22nd November, 2000, S.O. 1088(E), dated 11th October, 2002, S.O. 1569(E), dated the 19th September, 2006 and S.O.50(E), dated11.01.2010.

SCHEDULE {see rule 3(1) and 4(1)}
AMBIENT AIR QUALITY STANDARDS IN RESPECT OF NOISE

Area Code Category of Area/Zone	Limits in dB(A) Leq* Day Time	Night Time
(A) Industrial area	75	70
(B) Commercial are	65	55
(C) Residential area	55	45
(D) Silence Zone	50	40

Note:- 1. Day time shall mean from 6.00 a.m. to 10.00 p.m.

2. Night time shall mean from 10.00 p.m. to 6.00 a.m.

[24] [3. Silence zone is defined as an area comprising not less than 100 metres around hospitals, educational institutions and courts. The silence zones are zones which are declared as such by the competent authority].

4. Mixed categories of areas may be declared as one of the four above mentioned categories by the competent authority.

*dB(A) Leq denotes the time weighted average of the level of sound in decibels on scale A which is relatable to human hearing.

A "decibel" is a unit in which noise is measured.

"A", in dB (A) Leq, denotes the frequency weighting in the measurement of noise and corresponds to frequency response characteristics of the human ear. Leq: It is energy mean of the noise level over a specific period.

19. Inserted by Rule 8 of the Noise Pollution (Regulation and Control) (Amendment) Rules, 2010 notified vide S.O.50(E), dated 11.01.2010.
20. Inserted by Rule 2(ii)(a) of the Noise Pollution (Regulation and Control) Amendment Rules, 2006 notified vide S.O.1569 (E), dated 19.9.2006.
21. Substituted by Rule 9(i) of the Noise Pollution (Regulation and Control) (Amendment) Rules, 2010 notified vide S.O.50(E), dated 11.01.2010.
22. Inserted by Rule 9(ii) of the Noise Pollution (Regulation and Control) (Amendment) Rules, 2010 notified vide S.O.50(E), dated 11.01.2010.
23. Inserted vide Rule 2(ii)(b) of the Noise Pollution (Regulation and Control) Amendment Rules, 2006 notified vide S.O.1569 (E) dated 19.9.2006.
24. Substituted by Rules 4 of the Noise Pollution (Regulation and Control) (Amendment) Rules, 2000 notified vide S.O. 1046 (E), dated 22.11.2000.

www.ingramcontent.com/pod-product-compliance
Lightning Source LLC
Chambersburg PA
CBHW070814180526
45168CB00002B/617